PERFECT PRACTICE DRILLS

Basketball's Best Team Drills

Edited By Michael Podoll

Lessiter Publications, Inc. • Brookfield, WI

Publisher's Cataloging-in-Publication
(Provided by Quality Books, Inc.)

Perfect practice drills : basketball's best team drills /
edited by Mike Podoll
  p. cm.
  ISBN: 0944079-49-0

  1. Basketball—Coaching.   2. Basketball—Training
I. Podoll, Michael.

GV885.3.P47 2004   796.323'07'7
                           QBI04-200314

Edited by Michael Podoll
Cover and book design by Maureen Splitgerber
Cover Photo by Christopher Nielsen

International Standard Book Number: 0-944079-49-0

Published by Lessiter Publications, Inc.,
P.O. Box 624, Brookfield, WI 53008-0624.

For additional copies or information on other books or publications
offered by Lessiter Publications, write to the above address.

Telephone: (800) 645-8455 (US Only) or (262) 782-4480
Fax: (262) 782-1252 • E-Mail: info@lesspub.com
Web site: www.winninghoops.com

Manufactured In The United States of America

FOREWORD

Drill Selection Requires Thought, Planning

PRACTICE ORGANIZATION and the types of drills you use are critical toward getting your players to learn your offensive and defensive systems, as well as to improve their basketball skills and grow together as a cohesive team.

Drills have played a tremendous role in my development as a coach. Back in 1962, while I was getting my master's degree at Kansas State, Bill Guthridge and I took a class taught by Tex Winter, who was in the middle of putting together his famous triple-post book. Going through the book chapter by chapter is how I got many of the offensive drills that I've used throughout my career. Later on, I picked up some great practice-organization tips and drills from John Wooden at the old "7-Up" coaches clinics. This information was especially valuable and taught me the importance of being efficient with your drills (spending more than 10 minutes on drills is too long).

As the years went on, I accumulated more drills that fit into my system and style of coaching. I built up a repertoire of 5-on-5 drills from Sam Butterfield when I was at Hutchinson Junior College, some great defensive drills when I was a member of Eddie Sutton's staff and individual defensive drills from Boyd "Tiny" Grant (Fresno State) — just to name a few.

And the education never ends. To this day, I'm always on the lookout for clever drills from my coaching peers. Larry Brown, for example, is a master at developing drills that help players make smooth and quick transitions from offense to defense. I picked his brain for drills while we worked together for USA Basketball.

As you pour through the 160-pages of *Perfect Practice Drills*, you'll see creative drills from many excellent coaches at various levels of basketball. Here's one piece of advice ... before you begin to use a drill, make sure you understand the "key" to the drill and what carryover effect it will have on your offensive and defensive schemes. Ask yourself, "What's the purpose of this drill? How do I teach it to my players? Does it apply to what we're currently doing? And does this drill play to my team's strengths?" A drill shouldn't be used just because it looks good or because some famous coach invented it. The function of a drill is to get your players to improve the skills necessary for the team to succeed on the court. Drills can be boring and non-productive if they don't have a tangible carryover value to your games.

Enjoy the drills presented in the pages of this book. If you choose each drill wisely and take the extra time preparing how you're going to teach it to your team, you'll reap the rewards of confidence, better technique and aggressiveness from your players. Best of luck in your coaching journey and remember that learning never ends!

—*Gene Keady,*
Advisory Board Member,
Winning Hoops

COURT TERMINOLOGY, POSITIONS

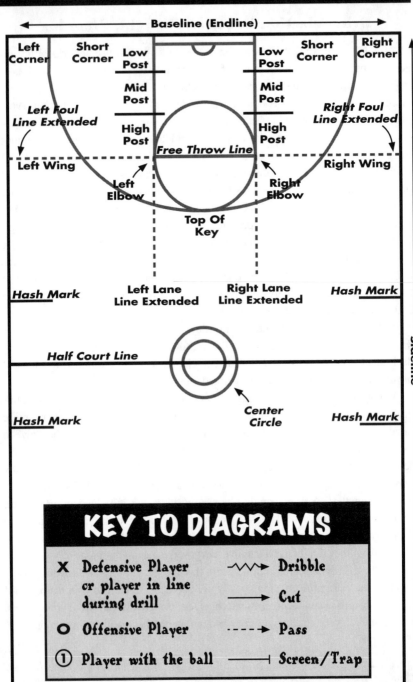

Baseline (Endline)

Left Corner | Short Corner | Low Post | Low Post | Short Corner | Right Corner

Mid Post | Mid Post

Left Foul Line Extended | Right Foul Line Extended

High Post | Free Throw Line | High Post

Left Wing | Right Wing

Left Elbow | Right Elbow

Top Of Key

Hash Mark | Left Lane Line Extended | Right Lane Line Extended | Hash Mark

Half Court Line

Center Circle

Hash Mark | Hash Mark

Sideline

KEY TO DIAGRAMS

X Defensive Player or player in line during drill

⟿ Dribble

O Offensive Player

⟶ Cut

① Player with the ball

----▸ Pass

⊢ Screen/Trap

8-PLAYER PASSING DRILL

By Will Mayer, Head Boys Coach,
Middletown High School, Middletown, N.J.

This is a great warmup drill that we use to get our practices off to a flying start. Players are partnered up into the following pairs: 4 and 8; 1 and 6; 3 and 5; 2 and 7. Players 4 and 8 each have a ball. All players pass to the right and sprint hard, following the pass and replacing their partner.

The players run this drill at top speed for 2 to 3 minutes. If the ball hits the floor at any time, the clock restarts from the beginning. This ensures that the passes are crisp, quick and accurate.

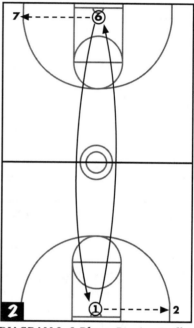

DIAGRAM 2: 8-Player Passing Drill (Continued).

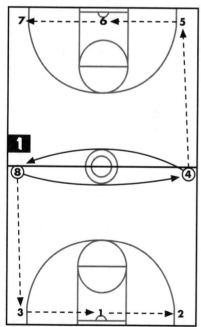

DIAGRAM 1: 8-Player Passing Drill.

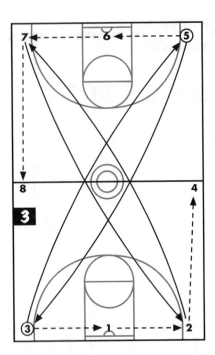

DIAGRAM 3: *8-Player Passing Drill (Continued).*

BONUS DRILL: CIRCULAR LAYUP DRILL

By Denny Van Sickle, Head Girls Coach
Onsted High School, Onsted, Mich.

THIS IS A GOOD drill to use before starting the second half since it packs a lot of activity into a short time.

Our team has 12 players and we use three balls in the drill. The diagram below shows the drill running in a counterclockwise direction, but it can be reversed, in which case B and D would switch jobs.

LINE A. This line has three players, each with basketballs. They form the shooting line.

LINE B. All the extra players are in this line, which feeds new players into the drill. B's job is to pass to A, then go to position C.

LINE C. Players here receive a pass, deliver a pass and move to Line D.

LINE D. Players here receive a pass, then pass to the shooter, follow the shooter to the basket and get the rebound. They then take the ball to the end of line A, where they will become the shooter when they reach the front of the line.

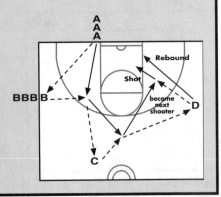

5-PLAYER WEAVE INTO TRANSITION

By Von Griffin, Head Boys Coach,
Bowling Green High School, Bowling Green, Ohio

This is an excellent drill for enhancing your team's offensive and defensive transition work.

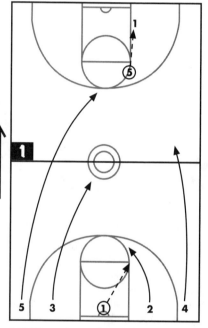

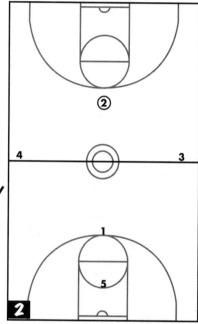

DIAGRAM 1: *5-Player Weave Into Transition.* The drill starts by having your players perform a fast 5-player weave downcourt to score a layup in transition. Both the passer and the player who makes the layup, become defenders (players 1 and 5 in this example).

DIAGRAM 2: *5-Player Weave Into Transition (Into 3-On-2).* The players quickly transition downcourt the other way, playing 3-on-2 (1 and 5 on defense). Either the shooter or the player who turns the ball over becomes the defender (player 3 in this case). The two defenders (1 and 5) become offensive players after the shot is taken.

DIAGRAM 3: *5-Player Weave Into Transition (Into 2-On 1).* Players 1 and 5 go downcourt 2-on-1 against player 3 (the player who either took the shot or turned the ball over).

The players who are not involved in

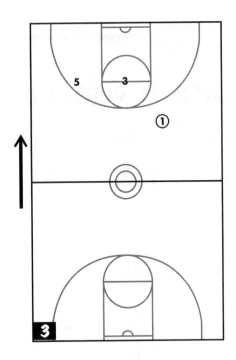

the 2-on-1 must sprint back on the outside of the court to the baseline and get ready to run the drill again. The coach decides on either a certain number of drill repetitions or a set time limit.

BONUS DRILL:
BUILDING A DEFENSIVE ATTITUDE

By Steve Robinson, Former Coach
Florida State University, Tallahassee, Fla.

GETTING PLAYERS TO think with a "defense first" attitude requires special practice competition. To instill this attitude, we developed the "Must-Stop-The-Competition Drill."

The drill starts in a half court setting and is played like a controlled full court scrimmage each time up and down the court. If the team that starts on offense scores, they get the 2 or 3 points they made and hustle back on defense.

If the defense stops them, the defense gets 10 points plus possession of the ball. The defensive team will bring the ball up the floor and run an offensive set. If they score they get the points and could easily be leading 12-0. At that point, we blow the whistle and ask the losing team whether they want to play offense or defense.

What do you think they say? It's always 'We want to play defense, coach.' It helps develop the attitude that they want to be on the defensive end of the floor.

We might play for only 3 minutes, but they play extremely hard defense the entire time. It also teaches them to take good shots on offense because they don't want to miss the shot and lose possession of the ball.

St. Joe's Progression Drill

By John Haas, Head Boys Coach,
L'Anse Creuse High School, Harrison Township, Michigan

Both our players and coaches love this transition drill that incorporates every basic odd-numbered break (2-on-1, 3-on-2, 4-on-3 and 5-on-4). Divide your squad into two teams (Team X and Team O in Diagrams) and send each team to opposite ends of the court.

Run this drill hard for 2 minute each practice, which equates to four or five full progressions.

court to play defense against two players from Team O in a 2-on-1 situation.

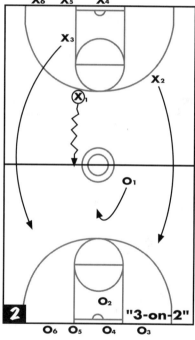

DIAGRAM 1: *2-On-1 Progression.* A player from Team X steps on to the

DIAGRAM 2: *3-On-2 Progression.*
After the shot goes up, the two players from Team O sprint back on defense and two players from Team X step on the floor and join the third player to go 3-on-2 going the other way.

DIAGRAM 3: *4-On-3 Progression.*
After team X puts up a shot, two more players from Team O step on the floor

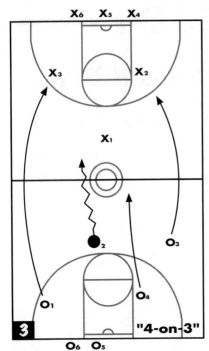

3 "4-on-3"

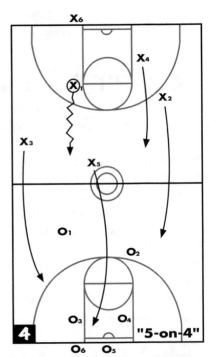

4 "5-on-4"

and the progression continues 4-on-3 going the other way.

DIAGRAM 4: *5-On-4 Progression.* The last portion of the progression has the 4 players from Team O taking a shot and sprinting back on defense, while two more players from Team X step on the floor, outlet the ball and go 5-on-4 the other way downcourt.

FULL-COURT COMBO DRILL WORKS PLAYERS HARD, DEVELOPS CRITICAL SKILLS

By Peter Harris, Head Mens Coach
Kansas City College And Bible School, Overland Park, Kan.

The following full-court combination drill gives your players a great workout while developing several critical skills simultaneously.

There are three big advantages to running this drill:

1. Your players will be kept moving, thinking and will not waste time.

2. Virtually all basic skills are practiced: dribbling, utilizing screens, working through screens, shooting, boxing out, rebounding, conditioning, defensive footwork, high-speed pressure layups, avoiding fouls, defensive denial, etc.

3. The coach has no ball-passing responsibilities and remains free to evaluate his or her players' skills and effort.

Have your players set up in four lines marked A through D.

❖ LINE A: Begins at the free-throw line with player 1 and extends diagonally toward the corner.

❖ LINE B: Begins near mid-court with player 2, and has the others in the line waiting near the sideline.

❖ LINE C: Begins at the opposite baseline corner, starting with player

3, with the others waiting in line out of bounds and along the baseline.

❖ LINE D: Begins at the far wing position on the same end of the court as line C.

Players 1 and 3 each have a ball and a chair is placed at the elbow above line C.

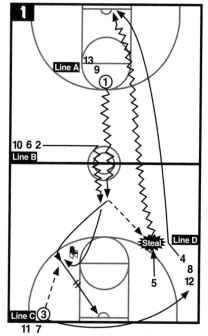

DIAGRAM 1: *Ultimate Full-Court Combo Drill.* 1 begins by dribbling

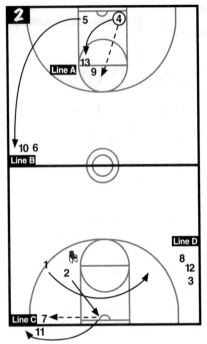

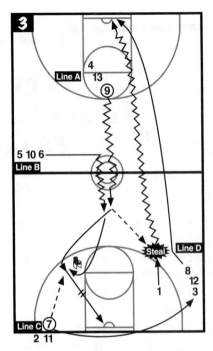

upcourt while 2 harasses him or her defensively, attempting to turn and stop 1 as much as possible. 1 continues to the top of the perimeter where he or she attempts to make a pass in the direction of 4.

5 must anticipate the pass, steal it and drive hard full court for the layup. (This is a perfect opportunity for players to gauge and improve their defensive quickness and ball close-out abilities). After the steal, 4 chases 5 and tries to prevent the layup without fouling.

After 1 has passed the ball, he or she breaks around the chair screen and receives a pass from 3 for the catch-and-shoot jump shot, while 2 defends.

DIAGRAM 2: *Ultimate Full-Court Combo Drill (Continued).* After shooting the layup, 5 goes to line B. 4

rebounds 5's layup, passes the ball to 9 and gets in line A.

On the other end of the floor, 2 boxes out 1, grabs the rebound, passes to 7 and gets in line C. 1, after shooting, becomes the wing defender (where 5 began the drill) and prepares to steal the pass that's about to be made from 9 to 8.

DIAGRAM 3: *Ultimate Full-Court Combo Drill (Continued).* The drill continues with the same patterns and motions as the players did in Diagram 1.

As your players become familiar with the drill, add a third ball to the action and have 9 begin dribbling immediately after 1 makes his or her initial pass. Another option is to have the coach set a realistic screen at the elbow instead of using a chair.

POST-UP STRONG DRILL

By Sam Priest, Head Boys Coach,
Ross Sterling High School, Baytown, Tex.

This is a great drill to get your players in the habit of moving quickly, improve their footwork and using proper post-up techniques.

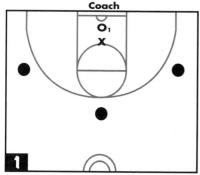

1

1 cuts in any direction.

2

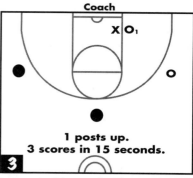

1 posts up.
3 scores in 15 seconds.

3

DIAGRAM 1: Player 1 is on offense and ad is facing the perimeter. X is the defender and is facing 1. There are three players set up on the perimeter, each holding a basketball. The team manager or coach is positioned on the baseline, under the basket.

DIAGRAM 2: On the coach's signal, 1 moves in any direction to get in front of the defender. The defender plays tough defense in an effort to keep 1 from getting into post-up position. Once 1 establishes post-up position, he or she receives an entry pass from the closest perimeter player.

DIAGRAM 3: Once 1 receives the pass, he or she must post up and score. The goal is for 1 to score three baskets in 15 seconds. The coach retrieves any rebounds or made baskets and throws the ball back to the player on the perimeter.

To spice up the drill, you may add defenders on the perimeter players who may double-down on entry passes. If you do this, you'll probably want to add additional time to the drill clock.

"BEAR DOWN" DRILL

By Purvis Dukes, Head Boys Coach,
Burke County High School, Waynesboro, Ga.

This is an effective and fast-paced defensive drill that teaches players how to get into good defensive position and draw charging fouls.

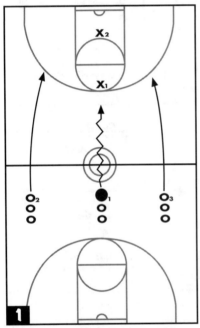

DIAGRAM 1: The drill begins with three lines of players set up at half court and two defensive players (X1 and X2) on one side of the floor. X1 is set up at the top of the key, while X2 is positioned in the middle of the lane. O1 has a ball and initiates the drill by dribbling down the middle of the floor. O2 and O3 streak downcourt on each side, simulating a 3-on-2 break.

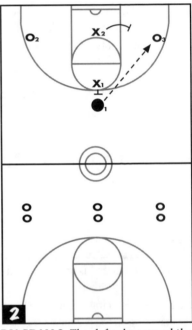

DIAGRAM 2: The defenders guard the 3-on-2 break and try to get into position to take a charge. The top defender (X1) must take a charge from X1 as he or she passes to a perimeter player. The bottom defender (X2) must slide toward the side that the ball is passed to and get into position to take a charge from the wing player who received the ball and is trying to drive to the basket for a layup.

The ball handler must come down the center of the floor and can use any type of dribble move he or she

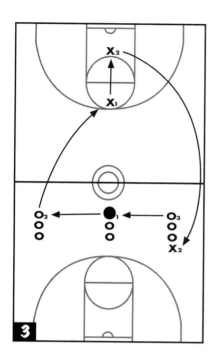

wishes to use. Allow only one pass. The player who receives the ball must try to score on a layup.

DIAGRAM 3: Players rotate clockwise after each repetition until everyone has been through the entire drill.

4-ON-4 CONTINUOUS DRILL

By Thomas Hammer, Head Girls Coach,
Westwood High School, Ishpeming, Mich.

This is an up-tempo combination drill that helps your team with defensive communication.

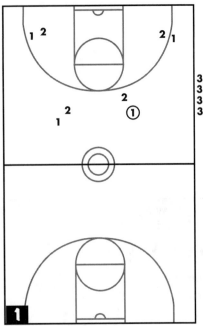

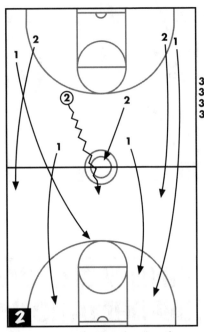

they execute a fast break going the other way.

DIAGRAM 1: Team 1 is on offense, while Team 2 is on defense. Team 3 is set up on the sideline and must be ready to get into the drill in a hurry. Team 2 plays defense until it either gets a defensive rebound or steal. If Team 1 scores, they stay on offense (make-it, take-it).

DIAGRAM 2: Once Team 2 secures a defensive rebound or steals the ball

DIAGRAM 3: When the shot is taken by Team 2 — whether it's a make or a miss — Team 1 runs off the floor and heads to the sideline. Team 3 sprints on the court and gets into defensive position. Team 2 brings the ball down on offense, tries to score on Team 3 and the drill continues.

Run the 4-on-4 drill for a set time limit or until a team scores a predetermined number of baskets.

This drill really helps improve your

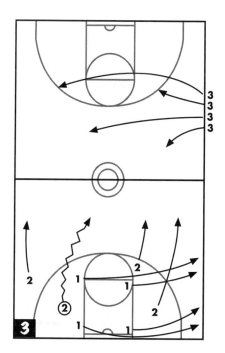

defensive communication, as players must shout out who they are responsibly for as they sprint out on to the court to play defense.

BONUS DRILL:
HELPING ATHLETES TO IMPROVE

By Daniel Brandel, Assistant Mens Coach
Oakland Community College, Waterford, Mich.

THERE'S NEVER ENOUGH practice time during the first few weeks in the fall to get your players enough reps, so having them work out individually is key. The following are things your players must work on during the off-season:

1. Footwork drills.

2. Ball-handling drills.

3. Two-ball dribbling drills.

4. Use a 3-to-1 ratio with your weak hand until both hands are equal.

5. Start practice with weak hand first. It helps maintain confidence and lets the workout end on a positive note.

6. Use bounce passes exclusively.

7. Always shoot close to the basket first and work your way out — never vice versa!

8. Never shoot less than 50 percent from the field in practice. Shoot layups (if you have too) to keep your percentage high.

9. Visualize doing the skill properly.

BENCH-SPRINTS DRILL

By Wayne Walter, Former Head Mens Coach,
Thaddeus Stevens College, Lancaster, Pa.

This fun and creative drill was designed because we were losing too much time during our time outs getting our players on and off the floor. This drill helps set up an organized regimen in a light-hearted, yet efficient manner.

You can modify the drill to match your bench decorum and league rules for time outs. We modify the drill when we're preparing for road games and we know that items, such as the water cooler, may be in a different area (especially if we've played there before). This drill is a fun way to end your practices.

DIAGRAM 1: *Bench-Sprints Drill.*

A. The drill begins with 5 players on the end of the floor opposite to your team's designated bench area, running through a pattern offense 5-on-0. At any time, the coach can call for a time out. On the coach's time-out signal, your players must sprint toward their bench and sit down in the first five chairs. This must be done in under 5 seconds.

B. Your entire coaching staff must huddle-up together in front of the

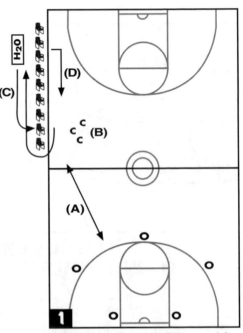

bench, but far enough outward for the players to get organized and seated. From time-to-time, mix things up by allocating that certain coaches need to go to the scorer's table, talk to an official, check up on a player's pseudo injury or check the score book.

C. The five bench players (either the second unit or a mix of first and second teamers) who were sitting in the first five seats, must sprint to the water station, get a cup of water and hustle to bring it to the players who are seated (and without spilling). They are to hand the water to the seated players from behind the bench.

D. The rest of the team must gather behind the coaches as they approach the seated five players and form a team huddle around the coaches and players.

Always be sure to use a different mix of players and change their roles during the drill, so that each player takes a turn as an "on-the-court" player, a "water bearer" and "huddle-forming" player, as these situations are continuously changing during the course of a game.

You'll be amazed at how much this simple, yet fun drill improves your time-out efficiency.

BONUS DRILL: PERFECT START TO PRACTICE

By Ken Seybold, Former Boys Head Coach
Flagler Palm Coast High School, Bunnell, Fla.

OUTLET DRILL. Half the team is positioned under the basket; the other half is stationed near the outlet area. The first player throws the ball off the backboard, grabs the rebound, makes an outlet pass and fills the lane.

The outlet player pushes the ball up the court and must decide whether to shoot or pass at the foul line.

After the pass or shot, that player rebounds the ball and makes the outlet pass. The players then run the drill in the opposite direction.

After all the groups have finished, run the drill at the other basket. Once again, let the next group go after the first group has reached half court. At the end of this drill, the players organize themselves into three-man groups.

WEAVE WITH JUMPER. Depending on your team, you might want to allow only three passes during this drill.

Players run a weave and on the third or fourth pass a jump shot is attempted. If the shot is missed, players have one chance to make the basket. If the ball is rebounded outside the lane, allow the players one dribble before they shoot again.

The player who grabs the rebound of the first shot and then makes a shot is to take the shot at the other end of the floor.

RECOVERY DRILL

By Bill Savarese, Head Boys Coach,
Murry Bergtraum High School, New York, N.Y.

The object of this drill is to get your players to improve their reaction time for getting back on defense and for quicker defensive recovery while in transition. It also incorporates your fast-break patterns, improves your players' decision-making abilities and skills such as boxing-out for rebounds, ball handling and shooting.

tioned across the court at the foul-line extended. The defensive players are numbered 5 through 1, going left to right.

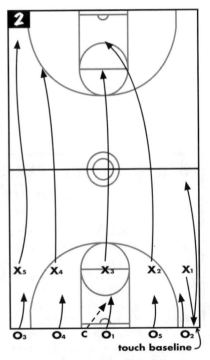

DIAGRAM 1: Line up five offensive players along the baseline and five defensive players opposite them, posi-

DIAGRAM 2: To begin the drill, the coach yells out a defensive player's number while rolling the ball out to an offensive player of his or her choosing (in this example the coach yelled "1," as signal for defender X1).

On the coach's yell, the offensive players secure the ball and head downcourt on a fast break. All the defenders run back in defensive transition, except for the defender who's number was called out by the coach (X1 in this example). This player (X1) must run and touch the near baseline before heading into defensive transition, giving the offense a momentary 5-on-4 break advantage. The called-out defender (X1) must touch the baseline and hustle back as fast as possible to help his or her teammates on defense. The offense tries to score in transition. **DIAGRAM 3:** On the shot attempt, the defense secures the rebound or quickly inbounds the made basket and heads back in transition coming downcourt the other way. Rotate in a new set of five players (if you have 15 on your roster) and run the drill again. Repeat the drill for set number of transition repetitions or for a pre-

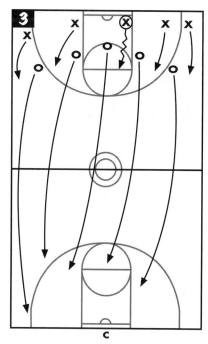

determined time limit. The coach must be sure to mix up the player he or she calls to touch the baseline.

"PAINT" DRILL COATS PLAYERS WITH HUSTLE, AGGRESSIVENESS

By Gary Williams, Head Mens Coach,
University of Maryland, College Park, Md.

The "Paint" drill is one that we use in the beginning of every practice to get things moving. It's a very physical, fast-paced and intense drill that improves your players' box-out ability, rebounding, outlet passing, defensive transition, fast breaks and is a great conditioner.

Competition is fierce in this drill, yet your players will enjoy it. As with most drills, in order to get the most out of it, the Paint drill must be run at game speed and under strict supervision by the coach.

Paint Drill

The drill begins with five offensive players (O's) lined up around the perimeter of the 3-point circle and paired off against five defensive players (X's) who are lined up opposite each offensive player, but inside the 3-point line. All players should be facing the basket. It doesn't matter where most position players line up, but your point guards (O1 and X1) must always stand at the top of the key. Three coaches or managers stand behind the groups of players, each holding a ball.

DIAGRAM 1: To start the drill, one of the three coaches or managers randomly shoots and intentionally misses a

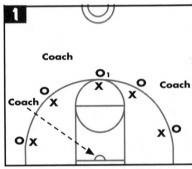

jump shot. The offensive and defensive players must battle for the rebound.

If an offensive player (O) secures the board, he or she tries to put the ball back up and score. Tip-ins are not allowed. An offensive player must secure the rebound, land with both feet and put up a strong, power move to score. The offensive rebounder can use head fakes, but must still go up aggressively with the put-back attempt.

Going up strong with the rebound gets your players used to game-like conditions for grabbing a rebound, putting up a shot, making the basket and drawing a foul for a 3-point play.

Transition Work

If a defensive player gets the rebound, that player throws an outlet pass to a teammate on the wing and the X's run a fast break to the other end of the court.

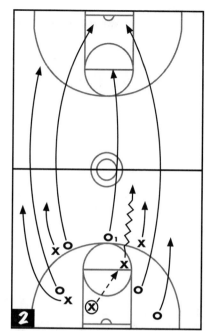

DIAGRAM 2: Once the X's begin their fast break, the O's must hustle back in transition and try to stop the score. If the O's stop the initial fast break, they must get back to defend the paint and set up into whatever type of zone or man defense you want them to apply. To improve team communication, have your point guard (O1) call out the defense during transition.

If the X's don't score on the fast break, they run a secondary offensive attack until either they score or the defense gets completely set up. Coaches blow the whistle to stop play and they set up to run the drill again.

Run the drill to a set a number of scored points or have a set time limit as the goal. Whatever team has the most points at the end of the time limit wins. "Punish" the losing squad with a brief period of conditioning work, push-ups or sit-ups. While the losing squad is fulfilling their punishment, "reward" the winning squad with passing, shooting and free-throw shooting drills.

Since this is a warmup drill, keep the reward-punishment phase extremely brief and well organized.

ELBOW SHOOTING DRILL

By Nate Webber, Head Boys Coach,
Notingham High School, Trenton, N.J.

This drill is used to create game-like situations where your players are constantly moving and placing themselves in proper position to shoot the ball.

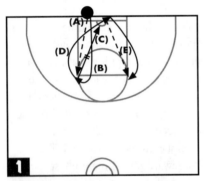

DIAGRAM 1: The drill begins by having a player who's holding a basketball positioned under the basket and facing the foul line. The player lobs the ball in the air toward the left elbow (A), sprints to the left elbow (B), catches the ball (either from the air or off one bounce) and shoots a jumper from the elbow (C).

The player then retrieves his or her own rebound (D) and lobs the ball toward the right elbow (E).

DIAGRAM 2: The player sprints after the lobbed ball, catches it while utilizing a jump stop, pivots to the left until he or she is square with the basket and shoots another jump shot, this time from the right elbow. It's important to make sure that when the player pivots,

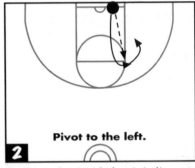

Pivot to the left.

that his or her inside foot is in line with the front of the basket.

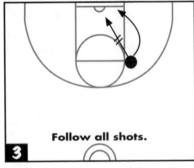

Follow all shots.

DIAGRAM 3: The player follows the shot and either retrieves the make or rebounds the miss. Once he or she secures the ball, the player must power up strong and put in layup.

DIAGRAM 4: The player grabs the ball as it comes to the net and tosses it back out toward the left elbow to begin the drill again. On the left elbow, it's important that the player utilizes a left pivot, until the inside

Pivot to the left.

4

5

foot is in line with the basket. Once the player's inside foot is in line with the basket, he or she shoots another jumper and the drill continues.
DIAGRAM 5: *Variation.* This drill should be done at game-like speed and

intensity for 20 consecutive shots or three sets of 10 shots at top speed. All rebounds or made jump shots must be followed up by having the player go up strong and make a power layup.

BONUS DRILL: HIGH-SPEED TRAPPING DRILL

By Bill Salyers, Program Director and Basketball Coach,
The Kingdom Crusaders AAU, Dayton, Ohio

IT'S ONE THING to walk through a press in practice, explaining positions and responsibilities to your players. But it's quite another to have to teach it from the sidelines in real-time basketball situations.

This is a drill that not only helps to teach the trapping technique, but also allows a coach to evaluate which of his or her players will get physical, who won't and who can handle the ball in traffic. This drill also teaches your defense the importance of continuous communication.

The coach is at half court with a ball. There are three lines of players starting with the offensive player along the sideline. Two other lines are defensive players and they should be arms-reach apart.
DIAGRAM: When the coach slaps the ball, all three players should break for the basket. The coach will pass the ball to the offensive player. Instruct the defensive players not to intercept the pass, at least initially. One of the defenders should take responsibility for the basket side of the trap and one player has responsibility for the "up-court" side of the trap.

When your team first performs this drill, initially restrict it to just one side of the court.

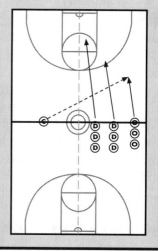

145 DRILL IS A GREAT WAY TO TEACH OFFENSIVE FUNDAMENTALS

By Jim Osborne, Head Womens Coach,
Haverford College, Haverford, Pa.

The 145 Drill (1-4 high set, 5 trips up and down the court) is a terrific drill for teaching your players basic offensive fundamentals such as spacing, transition, fast-break organization, V-cuts, meeting passes and is a great skill-based conditioner.

Initial Alignment, Basic Pattern

DIAGRAM 1: *Basic Pattern.* Have five players line up at half court with your point guard in the middle of the floor with a ball. On the coach's signal, players 2, 3, 4 and 5 sprint to the baseline, then to their assigned spots out of a 1-4 high set. 1 takes a few hard dribbles toward the basket and sets up near the top of the 3-point circle to initiate a quick-hitting play.

Once your players are at the designated spots, 1 calls out a play number and they quickly run the play. The fol-lowing diagrams show the assigned play and their corresponding number.

After each play is run, all five players return to half court and wait for the coach's signal. Run the plays in sequence and repeat. Once your players have run all five plays, add variations.

This drill can be timed or run for a designated number of sets. If you want to really make this drill a good conditioner, have the players sprint full court. Sprinting full court and quickly running a play is also a good way to simulate game-like situations.

Five Plays From 1-4 High Set

DIAGRAM 2: *"Give-And-Go" (Play No. 1).* 1 passes to 2, then comes off 4's screen and breaks to the basket. 2 passes to 1 for the layup.

Variation: 4 sets a ball screen for 1 who drives to the basket for a layup.

DIAGRAM 3: *"Backdoor" (Play No. 2)*. 2 makes a V-cut to the basket, 1 passes to 4 who passes to 2 for a layup.

Variation: Off the V-cut, 2 steps back for a 3-pointer.

DIAGRAM 4: *"Shoot A 3-Pointer" (Play No. 3)*. 3 makes a V-cut toward the basket, then pops out for a 3-pointer off the pass from 1.

Variation: 3 receives the pass and does a baseline drive for a layup.

DIAGRAM 5: *"Pick-And-Roll" (Play No. 4)*. 1 dribbles to left and curls off a solid ball screen set by 4. As 1 curls off 4, 4 rolls toward the basket. 1 hits 4 rolling to the basket with a bounce pass, chest pass or lob.

Variation: 1 dribble drives toward 4's screen, does a fake handoff to 4 and drives for a layup.

DIAGRAM 6: *"Post Up" (Play No. 5)*. 1 passes to 3. On the pass, 5 rolls to

the basket. 3 passes to 5 for a layup.

Drill Variation: On the pass from 3 to 5, instruct 5 to shoot a drop-step shot, hook shot, jump shot or step-back jumper.

After-Shot Responsibilities

After each play is called and the shot is taken, all five players have specific responsibilities.

❖ 1 sprints back to midcourt and awaits the pass from an outlet player.

❖ 2 goes to the outlet position on the right-hand side and awaits an outlet pass from rebounder.

❖ 3 goes to the outlet position on the left-hand side and awaits an outlet pass from rebounder.

❖ 4 battles 5 for the rebound and throws it to the closest outlet player.

❖ 5 battles 4 for the rebound and throws it to the closest outlet player.

1-On-5 Close-Out Drill

By Jim Montijo, Head Boys Coach,
Iver C. Ranum High School, Denver, Colo.

This defensive close-out drill has a coach on the baseline holding a basketball, a defensive player set up under the hoop in "help-side position" and five offensive players who are spaced evenly along the perimeter.

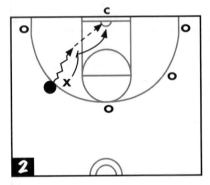

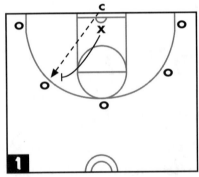

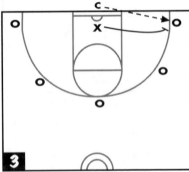

DIAGRAM 1: To start the drill, the coach throws a pass to any of the five offensive players. The defender must close-out hard on player who receives the pass.

DIAGRAM 2: The offensive player is allowed 3 dribbles to try to beat the defender to the basket. The two players go 1-on-1 until the offensive player scores or the defender gets a stop.

DIAGRAM 3: On any made basket or rebound the ball is handed back to the coach and he or she throws the ball back out to another offensive player. The defender must hustle over, close-out and the drill continues.

Running this drill for 2 minutes is physically demanding on the defender and is a great conditioner.

BREAK-IDENTIFICATION DRILL

By Len Garner, Head Boys Coach,
North Gwinnett High School, Suwanee, Ga.

This drill helps a team in transition identify mismatches, number advantages and defensive trailers. There are five offensive players set up in a half-court defensive position and a coach with a basketball positioned somewhere near them on the perimeter. The rest of the team (Xs) is standing behind the sideline on the far end of the floor with another coach.

As the ball is being rebounded, the coach who is with the sideline players sends 1 to 5 defensive players out on the court to defend the oncoming fast break. In this diagram example, the coach has sent two defenders out.

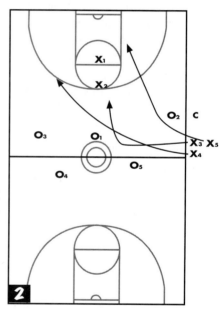

DIAGRAM 1: To start the drill, the coach shoots (intentionally missing) and the players on the court grab the rebound, throw an outlet pass and begin transition the other way downcourt.

DIAGRAM 2: The other three defenders cannot come out on the floor until the player with the ball has crossed halfcourt. You must really vary the numbers of players who come out to defend the break and also vary how hard to make the rebound carom, as these are critical components that may change the way the fast break is run.

3-ON-3 COMPETE DRILL

By Ron Twichell, Head Boys Coach,
Fort Zumwalt West High School, O' Fallon, Mo.

We like to run this drill at the end of every practice. It's competitive and the players love it. Place two coaches on the baseline and two coaches near half court. There are three defenders, ready to take on three offensive players. The rest of the team is distributed evenly along the three lines.

DIAGRAM 1: *3-On-3 Compete Drill.* The two teams play 3-on-3. The defense must force three consecutive stops. A stop is considered forcing a missed shot and securing the rebound, a steal, forcing a turnover, drawing a charging foul, etc.

The three defenders must stay in the drill until they get the three stops. If the offense scores, the next group of three step in and play offense. This

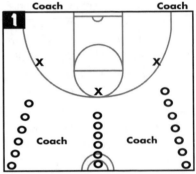

makes the drill extremely competitive and forces all players to compete at a high level. No group of three defenders wants to be embarrassed by being on defense for an extended period of time.

The coaches watch closely, officiating the 3-on-3, keeping score and calling any charging fouls.

HELP YOUR PLAYERS LEARN THE FUNDAMENTALS!

Rebounding *(24 pages)* $11.95

Every coach knows that rebounding is often the critical difference between having a very competitive team and one that's a perennial loser. This 24-page report features articles and drills from 23 outstanding coaches around the world. You'll find articles on offensive and defensive rebounding, rebounding tips, box-out techniques, coaching techniques, drills, securing missed free throws and preparing players for the mental aspect of battling for loose balls.

The Secrets Of Passing *(16 pages)* $9.95

Teach your players the art of passing the basketball with this outstanding coaching report. Written by some of today's top coaches, this report is filled with articles, drills and teaching techniques to improve your team's ball movement and to cut down on those aggravating turnovers. Articles include ways of teaching your players how to feed the ball into the post, developing good pass-catching hands, advanced passing concepts, improving your team's transition passing and 27 fantastic individual and team passing drills. Uncover all the hidden secrets of passing with this valuable report!

Stoppers!
Time-Tested Defensive Drills *(16 pages)* $9.95

Looking for rock-solid defensive drills that will turn your players into ball-hawking defensive stoppers? You'll get a proven 7-on-5 drill that prepares your players for live-game action, shell drills, a 3-on-3 drill sequence that teaches half-court man-to-man defense, drill games that spice up any practice, charge drills, help-side drills, defensive intensity and hustle drills, defensive transition drills, fundamental drills and much more! A comprehensive report for coaches who are looking for drills that will immediately improve their defenses.

Fundamental Dribbling *(8 pages)* $7.95

Read an exciting 8-page Special Coaching Report that contains right-to-the-point, highly valuable information from an outstanding high school coach that will definitely help your players improve their dribbling techniques. This in-depth ball-handling report details specific dribbling tips specifically aimed at individual players at every position, 13 moves to get away from defensive pressure, dribbling drills and more!

Ordering information...

Send your check or credit card information to:
Winning Hoops, P.O. Box 624, Brookfield, WI 53008-0624

FOR FASTER SERVICE, CALL: (800) 645-8455 (U.S. only) **or** (262) 782-4480

Fax: (262) 782-1252 • **E-mail:** info@lesspub.com • **Web site:** www.winninghoops.com

Wisconsin residents need to add 5.1 percent sales tax. Coaching Reports ship *FREE* to U.S. and Canadian customers.
Other foreign orders, add $2.50 shipping and handling for each report. Payable in U.S. funds drawn on a U.S. bank only.

Priority Code: WHPPD

"WILD-CARD" DRILLS

By Marty Cosgrove, Athletic Director and Head Girls Coach,
Sandwich High School, Sandwich, Mass.

As coaches, we are always encouraging our players to work on developing their skills. Many states have restrictive out-of-season coaching parameters. Without supervision and feedback, off-season skill development erodes into games of 5-on-5 pickup basketball.

"Wild Card Basketball" is a simple and effective way to get your players to work on skill development, communication, thinking skills and most importantly, team development. We created a deck of cards incorporating skills we wanted emphasized in 5-on-5 full- and half-court games.

Creation of Wild Card decks can be as simple as purchasing a package of lined index cards or as complicated as designing your own elaborate set of cards on your computer. The name of the drill or game is printed on one side of the card, while instructions are written on the back. Here are several examples of the cards we use to keep our players thinking team basketball during non-practice times.

❖ **"SUDDEN VICTORY."** The back of the card reads: "5-on-5 full-court game. No score is kept. All players on the team must score. After all 5 players score, the next point wins. In essence, a sudden-victory situation."

The rationale behind this game is to get everybody involved with scoring. Your players will now be looking for teammates, making the extra pass and helping other players get open. It also facilitates communication both on offense and defense. Your players will need to yell things such as "Who still needs to score?" and "We have to stop Suzie, she hasn't scored yet!"

❖ **"CONTINUOUS."** The back of the card reads: "5-on-5 full-court game, played up to seven points. When a team scores, they stay on offense, by getting the ball out of the net and attacking the defense in the other direction."

"Continuous" is an excellent conditioner and develops tremendous offensive and defensive transition skills.

❖ **"3, 5, 7."** The back of the card reads: "5-on-5 full-court game, played up to nine points. One point is awarded for all baskets, including 3-point shots. Teams may score from any area on the floor, however, on points 3, 5 and 7, the baskets must be 3-pointers. A team may score from inside the arc, but the score does not accumulate beyond 2, 4 and 6 until a 3-pointer is hit."

This game puts pressure on all players and increases defensive responsibility by forcing teams to extend their defense to the 3-point arc.

❖ **"DISCONTINUED DRIBBLE."** The back of the card reads: "5-on-5 full-court game, played up to nine points. Teams may dribble without restriction if they are in transition. However, if a team is in a half-court situation, no one may dribble inside the 3-point arc."

This game really helps develop screening, scoring off the screen and passing skills.

❖ **"POSTMAN."** The back of the card reads: "5-on-5 full- or half-court game, played up to nine points. There are no restrictions on offensive play, except that before a team may score, the ball must be entered to a post player."

This drill improves post player's passing skills (an often overlooked skill) and forces teams to slow down, knowing they can't score without a post entry.

❖ **"GOLDEN CHILD."** The back of the card reads: "5-on-5 full-court game, played up to nine points. There are no restrictions. Each team

has a player, who is selected as the golden child. All baskets are worth one point, however, the golden child's baskets are worth two points."

Defensive integrity and intensity increases on an individual and a team basis, as the "golden child" simulates that opponent who must be stopped.

❖ **"LEFTY."** The back of the card reads: "5-on-5 full- or half-court game, played up to nine points. All baskets are worth one point. All offensive entries must begin on the left."

"Lefty" is a simple game, but stresses the importance of utilizing both sides of the floor. Another added benefit is an increased comfort level of ball handlers working with their non-dominant hand.

❖ **"REWARD."** The back of the card reads: "5-on-5 full-court game, played to 13 points. All baskets are worth one point, as are any reward points for any skill a coach wants to emphasize."

Our team tends to reward points for offensive and defensive rebounds, but deflections, hustle points, (diving after loose balls, etc.) or a skill you want to emphasize, such as bank shots, could also be eligible for reward points.

"SEAHAWK" DRILL

By Steve Crous, Head Boys Coach,
Madison County High School, Danielsville, Ga.

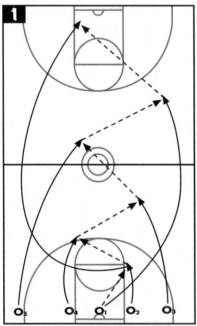

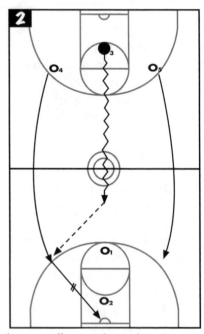

DIAGRAM 1: *"Seahawk" (5-Player Weave).* Start with five lines of players who run a 5-man weave downcourt. The last passer of the weave (O1 in this example) and the shooter (O2) get back on defense, while the other three players become offensive players and run a 3-on-2 break coming the other way.

DIAGRAM 2: *"Seahawk" (3-On-2).* As the 3-on-2 break comes downcourt, whoever takes the last shot or gets an offensive rebound gets back on defense and now the two defenders

become offensive players for a 2-on-1 situation.

DIAGRAM 3: *"Seahawk" (2-on-1 Into 1-on-1).* As the 2-on-1 break occurs, whoever takes the shot (O2 in this case) becomes a defender and that player (O2) must touch the baseline and then chase the player who secures the rebound or gets the ball as it comes through the net on a made basket (O4 in this case) and is going the other way for a 1-on-1 situation. After touching the baseline, the defender must hustle to catch up with

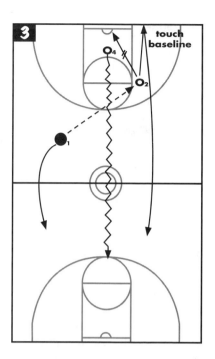

the offensive player (O4) who has a few steps head start.

BONUS DRILL:
NET MORE FREE THROWS IN PRACTICE

By Denny Van Sickle, Head Girls Coach
Onsted High School, Onsted, Mich.

BEGIN EVERY practice by having your players run laps, followed by these drills.

DRILL TO BEGIN PRACTICE. All players line up on the baseline. Select one player to step to the free-throw line and shoot twice.

If they miss both shots, the team (including the shooter) runs one full wind sprint* or suicide. If they make the first shot but miss the second, have your players run a half wind sprint. If they drain them both, the next shooter is selected and the first shooter does not run during the next wind sprint.

FOUL-SHOT DRILL. This drill incorporates free-throw practice with simple layup lines. Players line up and drive in hard, one at a time, for a layup. When they do, foul them solidly on the arm or body.

If they make the shot, they get 2 points. They then take the ball to another hoop and shoot either 1 or 2 free throws, depending on whether or not they made the layup (if they made the shot, they shoot only one).

Each free throw counts as 1 point. After each player has taken three layups, have them total their points (maximum is 9) and reward the winner as you see fit. You need several balls and at least three hoops to keep this drill running smoothly.

"PERFECTION" WARMUP TEAM DRILL

By Jim Johnson, Head Boys Coach,
Greece Athena High School, Rochester, N.Y.

This a great drill to begin your practices with. It gets your players immediately focused both mentally and physically. We usually do this drill once or twice a week before practice.

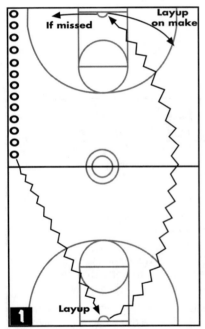

DIAGRAM 1: *Perfection (Phase 1)*. All players line up in a single-file line near the sideline and each player has a ball. On the coaches signal, one by one, each player goes full speed and makes a full-court, right-hand layup. If the player makes the layup, he or she then goes full court the other way and makes another right-hand layup. If a player misses either layup, he or she must return to the line and begin the drill again.

Once each player has made two right-hand layups, they switch the line to the opposite side of the floor and run the drill again, only this time they must make two consecutive full-court left-hand layups.

DIAGRAM 2: *Perfection (Phase 2)*. The players form two lines starting on the baseline with the lines spaced along each a lane line. The first two players in each line form a group and each pair of players must sprint downcourt, making crisp chest passes back-and-forth to one another. As they reach the other end of the floor, the last pass must be a bounce pass and the receiver must catch the bounce pass and make a layup. Each pair of players must go down and back without dropping a pass and they must make both layups or they have to get back in line and begin the drill again.

You can switch things up in this phase by calling out the type of passes you want to see the players make as

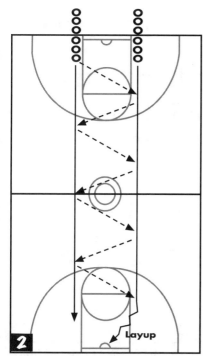

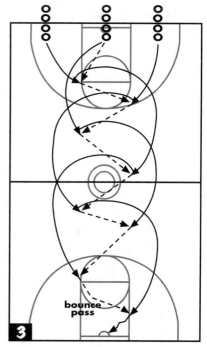

they head downcourt. Once each pair of players have completed Phase 2 perfectly, you move on to Phase 3.

DIAGRAM 3: *Perfection (Phase 3).* Phase 3 is a 3-player weave downcourt, utilizing the same rules as in Phase 2. The last pass must be a bounce pass that's caught and finished off with a made layup.

The first few times your team runs this drill, record the time it takes to run all three phases. Once a basic timeframe is determined, establish a set-time goal for your team to beat. As your players get better at the drill, raise the bar on the time limit. Players really enjoy the challenge of this drill.

3-ON-3 CLOSE-OUT DRILL (SEAL PENETRATION)

By Jason Graves, Head Boys Coach,
Ritenour High School, Saint Louis, Mo.

This drill is designed to improve your players close-outs and help-defense abilities. A coach is on the baseline with a ball, three offensive players are set up on top, while three defenders are spaced out along the baseline.

To begin the drill, the coach throws an inbounds pass to any of the three offensive players. The defender closest to the pass receiver must jump toward the ball and close-out hard.

The offensive players look to penetrate and score. Defenders must slide over, seal the penetration, get a hand in the shooter's face and block out for rebounds. If the defense makes a stop, they stay on the floor.

DIAGRAM 2: *3-On-3 Close-Out Drill (Example B).*

DIAGRAM 3: *3-On-3 Close-Out Drill (Example C).*

Scoring for the drill is as follows:

❖ OFFENSE: 1 point for any made baskets or successful penetrations to the basket.

❖ DEFENSE: 1 point for a successful seal penetration and rebound. 2 points for any drawn charges.

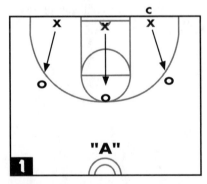

DIAGRAM 1: *3-On-3 Close-Out Drill (Example A).*

"WILDCAT" SHOOTING DRILL

By John Chapetto, Head Boys Coach, H.L. Richards High School, Oak Lawn, Ill.

This is a drill that helps improve shooting, post play and conditioning. Position three post players, who are lined up behind the baseline on each side of the floor. On one end of the floor, set up three shooters, spaced evenly along the perimeter and on the low block, set up one offensive post player with a post defender behind him or her.

behind the 3-point line. On the pass, the two post players on the low block (offense and defense) go "live" and begin to jockey for good post position anywhere in front of the basket.

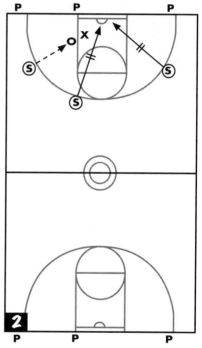

DIAGRAM 2: The perimeter player with the best angle and eye contact, makes an entry pass to the post player. As soon as the low-block post player puts up his or her shot attempt, the other two perimeter players shoot 3-point shots. The three players along

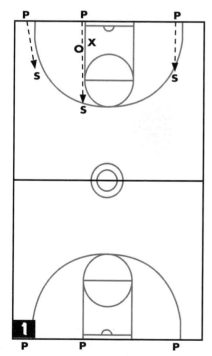

DIAGRAM 1: The baseline players pass to the three shooters who are

the baseline retrieve any rebounds or balls coming through the net on made baskets.

DIAGRAM 3: As soon as all the shots have been taken, the perimeter players must sprint and touch the near baseline, then run to the opposite end of the court, set up beyond the 3-point arc and receive a pass from the baseline players on that end of the court. All three shoot their 3-point shots and sprint to the other end of the floor for another repetition on the drill.

Run this drill continuously for 1 minute and then rotate positions until all the post and perimeter players have had their shots or until a predetermined set time limit has expired.

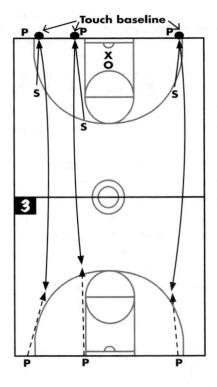

"21" DRILL

By Andy Cerroni, Head Boys Coach,
Sussex Hamilton High School, Sussex, Wis.

This is a great rebounding drill that also incorporates close-outs, ball screens, and both on- and off-the-ball defensive techniques. Divide your team into two even groups and name each group (we use "Red" and "Black"). One team starts on the base-line, while the other squad sets up behind the 3-point line at the lane-line extended. A coach stands under the basket and is holding a ball.

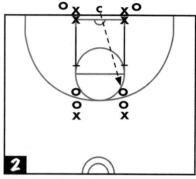

DIAGRAM 1: The coach begins the drill by passing to one of the players behind the 3-point line. The two defenders close-out quickly. One defender guard on-the-ball and the other closes-out on the off-the-ball player.

DIAGRAM 2: The players go 2-on-2 until either the offense scores or the defense gets a stop. The defense gets awarded a point for any steal or rebound of a missed shot. The offense gets a point for a basket, for drawing a foul of any kind and gets 3-points for any offensive rebound.

Switch from offense to defense and the first team up to 21 total points wins — the losing squad runs laps.

This is a very competitive drill. You can adjust the rules to make things even more competitive. For example, we do not allow our players to rebound their own missed layups.

7-ON-5 DRILL

By Chris Kusnerick, Head Boys Coach,
Rock Falls High School, Rock Falls, Ill.

This is a very good drill that our team uses throughout the year to help players improve their ability to play solid, team-orientated zone defense.

This highly competitive drill takes only 5 to 7 minutes to run and there is an offensive or defensive winner at the end of the drill. The losing team runs one sprint for each point difference between the two sides.

7-On-5 Initial Alignment

While this drill can be run using virtually any zone defense, it is shown here using a 1-2-2 zone defense (which our team primarily uses).

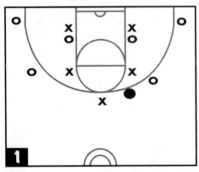

DIAGRAM 1: *7-On-5 Drill Using 1-2-2 Defense.* Start out with five players on defense using a 1-2-2 set (or whatever zone defense your team primarily uses). Align seven offensive players in the spots shown. Start out with five

offensive players on the perimeter and one on each block.

The drill begins with a checked possession at the top of the key.

7-On-5 Scoring System

The only way the defense can score is if they force a turnover or deflect the ball out of bounds. They get 1 point for each turnover forced or a deflection out of bounds.

Offensive players can't move on the inside or on the perimeter until a shot is taken. They also are not allowed to dribble, but can shoot at anytime.

The offense scores 1 point for each basket made and are allowed to go to the offensive boards after a shot attempt.

Play continues until the defense gains possession of the ball. Set a time limit and keep score.

DIAGRAM 2: Defensive players follow the proper defensive rotation princi-

ples based on where the offense is swinging the ball. Remember, the offense can't dribble to break down the zone, so defenders must react and rotate to cover the passes and movements of the ball.

This diagram shows the proper rotation of the defenders when the ball is passed into the corner.

DIAGRAM 3: Due to the fact that they are outnumbered on the perimeter and must also account for two offensive players on the blocks, defenders must react quickly on all cross-court skip passes.

This diagrams shows the proper rotation of the defenders when the ball is passed to the other side of the court.

Encourage Aggressive Play

This drill forces the defense to play very hard, which all coaches want on defense. Because the only way the defense can score is by a forced turnover or deflection, the drill encourages your zone defenders to play aggressively and take chances. They must also talk and communicate on defense at all times.

Coaches must call fouls very liberally. Every three fouls on the defense counts as a point for the offense team. Defenders must constantly pressure the ball, trap the corners and contest all shots.

Versatile Drill

Even though this drill is shown vs. a 1-2-2 defensive set, it can also be adapted for teams who play 2-3 zone or a flat 3-2 zone defenses. The rationale is if your defense can guard seven offensive players in this drill, they'll be more prepared to guard five players in live-game situations.

MONSTER DRILL

By Shaka Smart, Assistant Mens Coach,
University of Akron, Akron, Ohio

This drill develops the post defense and offensive skills of your players regardless of position. With no where to hide and no weak-side help two players must fight for position and then play 1-on-1 when the ball is entered into the post.

This drill is an extremely competitive and exhausting drill. Fatigue makes cowards of us all — but you'll see which players on your team fight through the exhaustion and which ones simply give up. Nonetheless, all your players will benefit from working on post offense and defense, both with and without the ball.

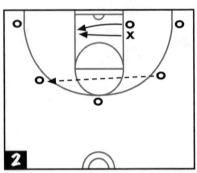

position, then attempts to keep the offense from scoring once the ball is entered. Conversely, the goal of the offense is to seal the defender, receive the ball deep in the post and score.

The passers are allowed to only make direct passes into the post and cannot throw lobs. As the ball is moved around the perimeter, each player tries to beat the other to the spot and stay low in order to maintain position.

Your players quickly learn the lesson that scoring position is won or lost before the ball arrives. Upon entry into the post, the play is live.

After a score or defensive rebound, the ball is outletted to the perimeter and the battle resumes. The drill continues for 60 seconds, after which defense goes to offense and a new defender steps in. Keep track of which player scores the most points and who gives up the least points. Call out for different matchups to keep things interesting.

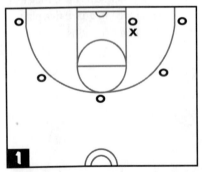

DIAGRAM 1: Start the drill with four or five players spread around the 3-point line and have two players in the post — one on offense and the other on defense.
DIAGRAM 2: With the ball moving around the perimeter, the defense tries to deny entry into prime post

"DAILY DOZEN" DRILL

By Dr. Greg Williams, Head Boys Coach,
North Hall High School, Gainseville, Ga.

This is a great drill to either begin or finish practice with each day. The object of the drill is to make 12 consecutive layups without the ball touching the floor or without committing a turnover.

Split up you post players into two groups and position them under each basket. Do the same with your guards and wings and place each group at the half-court line on each sideline. Put 2 minutes on your scoreboard's clock. DIAGRAM 1: Start the drill by having a coach toss the ball off the backboard, a post player grabs the rebound and throws an outlet pass to the guard or wing player who is breaking to proper outlet position.

The outlet player passes cross-court to the other guard or wing player, who is streaking downcourt for a layup. The post player who grabbed the initial rebound runs downcourt trailing the play and can tip in any missed layup.

The players must make 12 layups in a row before the 2 minutes expire off the scoreboard clock. If the trailing post player makes a tip-in, the count stays alive. If any player misses a layup, a tip-in attempt or a violation occurs (such as a turnover or any dribbling), the layup count starts over

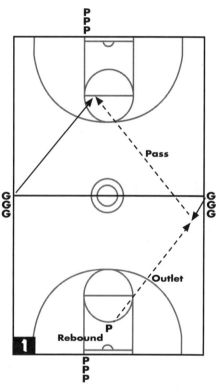

again back from zero. The clock, however, continues to run and is not reset.

If the time expires and the required 12 layups aren't met, you player must run sprints for however many layups they had left to reach the goal.

Players must communicate, hustle and stay positive to achieve their goals. This drill builds team unity and teaches your players not to panic under pressure situations.

FULL-COURT REBOUNDING DRILL

By Bill Ayers, Head Boys Coach,
Mt. Spokane High School, Mead, Wash.

This drill is continuous and stresses conditioning, as well as reinforces proper rebounding technique for both offense and defensive rebounders.

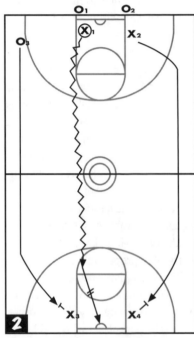

DIAGRAM 1: This drill begins with O1 dribbling to either elbow to and shooting a jumper. After taking the shot, the shooter does not rebound, but instead leaves the court. O2 and O3 run the lanes wide and angle toward the basket to grab the offensive rebound. X1 and X2 meet them just outside the lane and box out. The four players fight for the rebound.

DIAGRAM 2: Whoever of the four players — offense or defense — successfully secures the rebound (X1 in this Diagram), he or she dribbles downcourt and becomes the shooter on the opposite end of the floor.

The player whose opponent grabbed the rebound, stays on the court and runs hard, filling the lane wide going the other way downcourt (O3 in this Diagram). The teammate of either the offensive or defensive player who successfully secured the rebound, gets to leave the court (O2 in this Diagram). The player on the team who "lost" the rebound, fills the lane wide on the opposite side of the floor (X2 in this Diagram) and sprints hard downcourt.

DIAGRAM 3: In this Diagram, after X1's jumper, X3 has grabbed the rebound and power dribbles down-court going the other way. X2 gets to leave the drill because the defensive rebounder (X4) to his or her side did not get the board. O3 has to stay in the drill and run back downcourt in transition because the person to his or her side was the one who grabbed the rebound (X3).

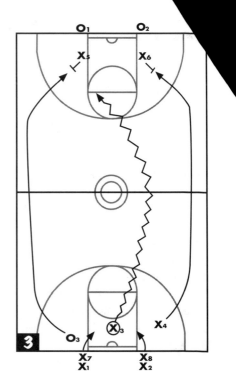

Two Ball-Handling Drills

By Tom Crean, Head Mens Coach,
Marquette University, Milwaukee, Wis.

Here are two great drills to work a wide variety of dribble moves such as the hesitation, the stutter dribble, stutter crossover, a pull-back dribble and the speed dribble, while under physical contact of a tough defender. It's best to run these drills while your players are fatigued so they'll get reps at performing dribble moves while tired and under pressure, which is what happens at the end of close games.

Line up your players in a single file line near the sideline at half court. Set up a coach, a chair or a cone in the areas indicated by the diagram. Managers or coaches are preferable to add a physical defensive element to the drill, which represents beating half-court pressure and help defenders.

DIAGRAM 1: *Dribble Series Drill.* The first player in line has a ball, takes a few dribbles and attacks the defender near halfcourt. This player dribbles head-on and directly toward the defender, forcing him or her to backpedal. As the ball handler gets to the defender, he or she attacks the backpedaling defender's shoulder, puts a dribble move on (whatever move you call for, such as a "hesitation" dribble, etc.) and goes around the defender. This teaches your players how to attack a defender in the

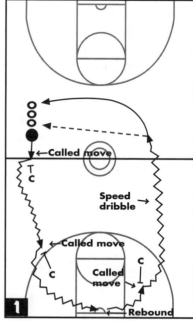

open floor.

As the ball handler approaches the 3-point line, a defender (coach or manager) who's positioned just inside the 3-point circle steps out and defends the ball handler. The ball handler attacks the defender and uses the same called move to get around him or her and drives to the basket, making a layup.

The ball handler grabs his or her own rebound as it comes through the basket and then power dribbles upcourt, as if clearing the rebound out, and puts a dribble move on the last defender who's positioned just outside the elbow.

After the ball handler clears the last defender, he or she power dribbles all the way back to the end of the line. After all the players have performed the drill, move the drill to the opposite side and have them perform dribble moves from the other side of the floor. Last, you can run a repetition of the drill with the players coming down the middle of the floor.

This drill gets your players three repetitions of a type of dribble move in one drill. To get maximum benefit from the drill, have your players run it at full speed and with great intensity. Make sure the players' dribbling is disciplined and don't tolerate sloppy ball handling.

DIAGRAM 2: *Explosion Drill.* This drill is similar to the previous drill except the intensity is turned up a notch and fatigue and contact come into play. The drill begins with O1 lining up at Spot 1. The coach who's underneath the hoop passes the ball to O1 and he or she power dribbles to the basket and makes a layup while getting bumped by a coach who is set up in the lane and holding a blocking pad. O1 grabs the ball as it comes through the hoop and throws it back to the coach underneath the basket. O1 quickly lines up and repeats the same process at Spots 2 and 3.

Important Note: The diagram shows the drill as it's in progress from Spot 4. It does not show the layups from Spots 1, 2 or 3.

When O1 gets to Spot 4 at halfcourt, he or she sprints downcourt

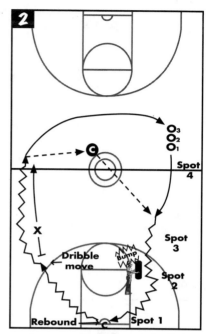

receives a pass from the coach who's positioned at halfcourt. The sprinting player catches the pass and dribbles at full speed toward the basket, puts a dribble move on the lane defender (taking the bump from the pad in the process) and makes a layup. After this fourth layup attempt, the player secures the rebound and speed-dribbles toward the defender on the opposite side of the floor. The ball handler uses the required dribble move and goes 1-on-1, trying to shake the defender all the way to halfcourt. Upon reaching halfcourt, the ball handler throws the ball back to the coach and sprints back to the end of the line.

Again, emphasize speed, toughness, precision and proper ball handling. Get the entire team more reps by running the drill simultaneously at both ends of the court.

11 PLAYER DRILL

By Bruce Reece, Head Girls Coach,
Madras High School, Madras, Ore.

This is a 3-on-2 continuous drill that teaches multiple skills such as rebounding, transition offense and defense, outlet passing and conditioning. Align the players as shown in Diagram 1. The rebounder or player who secures the loose ball is always on offense.

court and come down on a 3-on-2 transition situation versus two of the defenders (X1 and X2 in this Diagram).

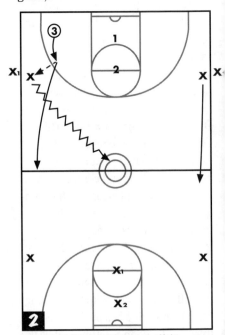

DIAGRAM 1: *11 Player Drill.* Start with two players on defense at both ends. Have an outlet line positioned on each sideline at the free-throw line extended. Three offensive players (1, 2 and 3 in this Diagram) set up at half

DIAGRAM 2: *11 Player Drill (Continued).* The player who gets the ball (3 in this Diagram), throws an outlet pass to the nearest outlet player and they begin a 3-on-2 transition going the other way. The outlet player who receives the pass fills the middle, while the rebounder (3) and other outlet player (X) run wide in transition.

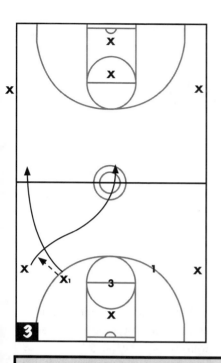

The two other original offensive players (1 and 2) stay back and become defenders, while the other two player (X1 and X2) sprint to the sideline at the foul-line extended and become the new outlet-pass receivers. DIAGRAM 3: *11 Player Drill (Continued)*. The drill runs continuously for a predetermined set time limit.

BONUS DRILL: "QUICK-FEET" DRILL

By Raymond Townsend, Retired Basketball Coach
Menlo College, San Jose, Calif.

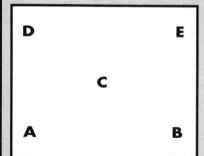

THIS DRILL GREATLY IMPROVES agility and is especially good for big men. Each component of the drill should be done continuously, with no rest between the exercises.

Set-up the pattern shown here on the floor and do the exercises described below. This drill should take about 25 minutes.

1. UP AND BACK
- ❏ Place feet on points A and B.
- ❏ Jump to C with both feet.
- ❏ Jump and place feet on points D and E.
- ❏ Without turning, repeat the process backwards.
- ❏ Repeat the cycle for 10 up-and-backs.

2. RIGHT FOOT
- ❏ Start on B and jump to C on right foot only.
- ❏ Go to D, E, C, A and B in that order and repeat 10 times.

3. LEFT FOOT
- ❏ Start on B, go to C, D, E, C, A and B in that order. Repeat 10 times.

4. BOTH FEET
- ❏ Follow the same pattern as for left-right foot. Repeat 10 times.

"444" OR "555" DRILL

By Marty Gaughan, Head Boys Coach,
Benet Academy, Lisle, Ill.

Split your team into three separate teams. Each team consists of either four or five players (depending on either the size of your roster or specific needs). For this drill, you should separate the squads or modify the drill into specific defenses, offenses, special situations, etc. You can also include full-court pressure, for example, where a team needs to attack one team in the backcourt and then attack the next team in the front court.

This drill is extremely competitive and is effective for working on different offenses and defenses.

DIAGRAM 1: *4-on-4-To-4 Example.*
DIAGRAM 2: *5-on-5-To-5 Example (Full-Court Press, To Attacking Half-Court Pressure).*
DIAGRAM 3: *5-on-5-To-5 Example (Set Offense Vs. Man, To Attacking A 2-3 Zone Defense).*

Add a point system into the drill and reward extra points to the team who executes the things that you need to do against your next opponent. For example, we'll reward 5 points for

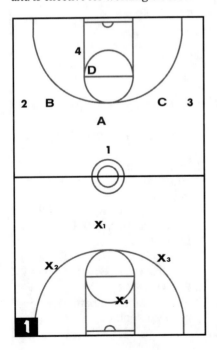

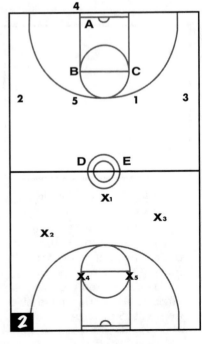

offensive rebounds if we're going to be facing a team that we think we can effectively rebound against.

Take away points for any team who commits a turnover (especially if you're going to be facing an opponent who's known for forcing turnover) or fouls.

This drill allows you an opportunity to switch players to different units for different scenarios and see which lineups work best and which ones are most effective for a particular situation.

You can also easily modify this drill to incorporate things such as a possession beginning with an out-of-bounds pass or free-throw attempt (off a make or miss).

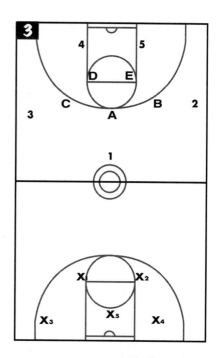

TWO OFFENSIVE & DEFENSIVE POST DRILLS

By Joe Pitt, Head Boys Coach,
Union High School, Union, S.C.

DIAGRAM 1: *Post Drill.* This is a terrific drill to teach scoring in the post and defending the post in a reactionary movement. Place an offensive player on each low block and a defender in the middle of the lane. A coach stands on the top of the key, holding a basketball.

The coach begins the drill by passing to either offensive post player. The post player who receives the pass must go straight up and try to score (no head fakes are allowed). The defender must react defensively, slide over and try to block the shot.

DIAGRAM 2: *Vimp Drill.* This is a great drill for teaching players how to defend flash cutters and how to play 1-on-1 defense in the post. Set up an offensive player on each low block and an offensive player set up wide on each wing. A defender is placed in the middle of the lane and a coach stands at the top of the key, holding a basketball.

The coach passes to either wing. As this occurs, the ball-side post drops off the court and the backside post flashes to the ball. The defender works hard to deny the flash cutter the ball. If the entry pass is made the two play 1-on-1. Rotate players into each position.

"THREE-DOWN" SHOOTING DRILL

By Bill Agronin, Head Womens Coach,
Niagara University, Niagara, N.Y.

To improve your team's 3-point shooting, you can use this drill any time during practice. We've found it to be most effective at the end of practice. The players like it because it's a competitive drill and there is a goal to be met. Coaches like it because the drill emphasizes shooting, conditioning, squaring up before shooting and making a good passes.

You need a minimum of nine players to run this drill, but it's ideally run with 12 players.

DIAGRAM 1: Begin with three players on each baseline and three players positioned at half court. Each player on the baseline has a ball. Have a coach or team manager stationed on each end of the court to keep score.

DIAGRAM 2: The players from half court run toward the baseline. As the half-court players run toward the baseline, the players on the baseline pass the ball to the oncoming players and

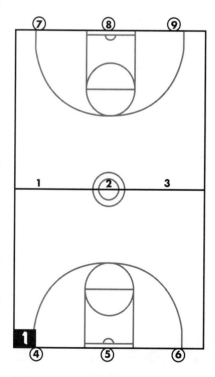

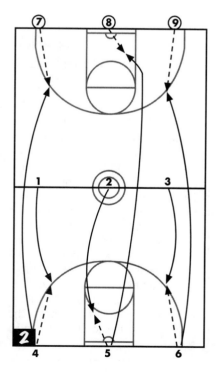

then sprint toward the opposite basket. The three sprinting players receive a pass from the baseline players.

The sprinting players must shoot as soon as they receive the pass from a player on the baseline. A 3-point shot is worth 3 points, a jumper inside the 3-point line is worth 2 points and any shot in the paint is worth 1 point. Limit 3-point shot attempts to your better shooters — all others should shoot inside the arc.

The drill continues for 1 minute and if the team scores a predetermined number of points — then the drill is over. If the set score is not achieved, the players must repeat the drill.

We begin our season with a goal of 60 total team points in 1 minute. As the season progresses, we bump up our goals to 65, then 70 points. Each shooter must get his or her own rebound and must be ready to pass to the next group of three coming downcourt.

BONUS DRILL:
OFFENSIVE REBOUNDING DRILL

By Bill Wenning, Boys Basketball Coach
Cushing Academy, Ashburnham, Mass.

THIS DRILL EMPHASIZES toughness, commitment and conditioning.

DIAGRAM: Start with three players (1, 2, 3) in the paint and the rest of the team lined up under the hoop. The coach will throw the ball off the backboard at that point the ball is live until the end of the drill. All three players will attempt to rebound the ball and score. Once a player scores, he or she goes to the end of the line and the next player (4) steps onto the court.

As the ball goes through the hoop, it's still live and the next player in line runs in and joins the other players in the paint to fight for the rebound and attempt to score. The only way to get out of the drill is to score.

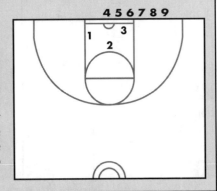

FULL-COURT, V-CUT DRILL

By Keith Cooper, Head Mens Coach,
St Martin's College, Lacey, Wash.

All coaches are aware of the importance of getting practice off to a good start. One of the best drills we've used to ensure a good start to practice is the full-court, V-cut drill.

This is a drill designed to incorporate multiple offensive fundamentals into a full-court drill in a short period of time. Once your players learn how to correctly do the drill, it usually takes only 10 minutes from start to finish.

Some of the fundamentals that are covered in the full-court, V-drill are:

❖ V-cutting
❖ Coming to meet passes
❖ Communicating
❖ Timing
❖ Pivoting
❖ Passing
❖ Dribbling, dribble moves
❖ Layups, jump shots
❖ Backdoor passes, backdoor cuts

How The Drill Works

The drill begins with players evenly distributed in four lines — labeled A, B, C and D — with each player in line A holding a basketball.

DIAGRAM 1: *Full-Court, V-Cut Drill.* The first player in line B executes a V-cut downcourt and comes back to receive a pass from player A. Stress to

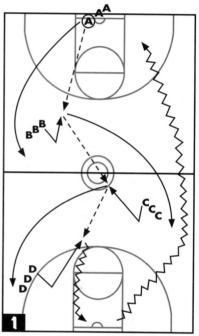

the players in line B that they must aggressively come back to meet the pass.

After receiving the pass, player B uses a front pivot and passes to the first player in line C without traveling. Player C also uses a V-cut and breaks hard to meet B's pass.

COACHING POINT: Attention to detail in practice, focusing on skills such as proper V-cuts and pivoting will save many turnovers when pressure defense is applied in a live-game situation.

Communication, Timing Is Critical

To get your players in the habit of communicating, have your players constantly making verbal calls throughout the duration of the drill, with the passer calling out the receiver's name and the receiver calling out the passer's name.

One of the keys for good timing in this drill is to have the next player in line begin his or her V-cut while the ball is in the air and going toward the player who will become the passer.

All passes (except for backcut, backdoor or post-entry passes) should be crisp chest passes.

After passing, players run to the end of the next line. The first player in line D will rebound any misses and use a power layup off both feet to finish the play. After making the shot or follow-up shot, player D will grab the ball as it comes through the basket and speed dribble the length of the floor, outside of line C, and shoot the appropriate shot at the other hoop. To keep things at a good pace or to mix things up and keep the players alert, have the coach call out or set up a sequence for the type of shot that your players in line D are to use (speed layup, reverse layup, pull-up jump shot, etc).

If player D misses the shot, he or she rebounds and follows it up with a power layup off both feet. The next player in line A takes the ball as it comes through the net and passes to the next player in line B, who is making the V-cut move toward line A.

As the drill progresses, the sequence of shots for the players in line D should be:

1. Speed layup.

2. Reverse layup.

3. Catch-and-shoot jump shot.

4. Pull-up jump shot after a crossover dribble.

5. Catch-and-shoot 3-point jump shot.

6. Return pass to C for a 3-point jump shot from the top of the key.

7. Return pass to C at the top of the key. D then posts up on the opposite low block and C dribbles over to get a wing-to-low-post passing angle.

8. Hard dribble by C directly at D, which is D's signal to execute a backcut and look for a backdoor bounce pass from C.

The first player up in line A is called the "change-it" player and when he or she gets back into the first-position spot in line A, it's time to change to the next shot in the sequence. Shoot each shot twice.

"22-8" DRILL

By Ray Kues, Head Girls Coach,
Bishop Brossart High School, Alexandria, Ky.

Throughout practices, we try to incorporate new and innovative ways to simulate game situations, especially drills which involve thinking skills as well as basic basketball skills. Too often, coaches neglect the mental aspect of basketball and expect players to master this part of the game without prior practice.

A few seasons ago, we developed a new drill called "22-8" or "Lady Stangs" (our mascot is the Mustangs). It has become one of our most productive drills and we run it at least twice a week in practice. Our players really get up for this drill and always give 100 percent effort.

By changing the scoring parameters slightly, this drill gives your players a great workout and helps them improve their skills on offense, defense, rebounding, screening and free-throw shooting.

How It's Run

The drill divides the teams into two evenly separated groups according to ability. One team plays offense for 8 minutes (or whatever time you find appropriate), while the other team plays defense for those same 8 minutes. The roles are reversed during the second 8 minutes.

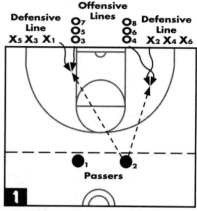

DIAGRAM 1: *"22-8" Initial Action.*
O1 and O2 are the initial passers and are lined up near half court. Either O1 or O2 pass the ball to O3 or O4 within the 3-point line. X1 and X2 defend the pass and play defense if the pass is completed.

The teams play 2-on-2 until a basket, defensive rebound or turnover occurs. Once the two offensive players have finished, they must run out to half court and pass to the next two offensive players who start underneath the basket and are guarded by two new defenders.

DIAGRAM 2: O1 and O2 return to the offensive line after the pass is completed. X1 and X2 return to the end of the defensive line after 2-on-2 is completed. O3 and O4 run near half court and either O3 or O4

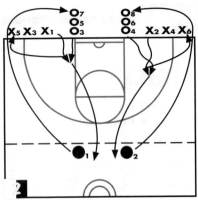

passes the ball to O5 or O6 who are being defended by X3 and X4.

After the pass, the two passers return to the offensive line. This continues for 8 minutes for each team.

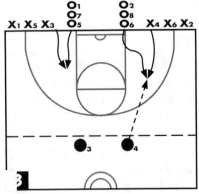

DIAGRAM 3: O3 and O4 attempt to pass to either O5 or O6 behind the 3-point line. X3 and X4 become the defenders.

O3 and O4 return to the offensive line after the pass and X3 and X4 return to the defensive line.

Scoring System

Keep track of the score and time on the scoreboard during the full 16 minutes of this drill so your players know how far they are ahead or

behind. Both the offensive and defensive teams can score.

The scoring system for the "22-8" drill is as follows.

Offensive Scoring: Points are awarded for baskets made. One point is awarded for a field goal, two points for a 3-point field goal and two points for every offensive rebound.

Defensive Scoring: The defensive team can score points by causing a turnover (two points) or denying the initial pass for 5 seconds (three points).

Drill Rules

Instruct your players that every initial offensive pass must be made inside the 3-point line or be considered a turnover. This makes it a bit tougher to get open instead of just running out to the passer. The offensive player may dribble outside the 3-point line, but only if he or she gets the initial pass without a turnover.

Emphasize to your players that good passes from out of bounds are just as important as the players who are working to get open. Stopping an inbounds pass for 5 seconds should be recognized as a great accomplishment and should be rewarded with three points.

Also instruct your players to use picks and screens as often as possible to keep the defense honest, as well as to encourage teamwork between the two offensive players.

"BANGER" OFFENSIVE REBOUNDING DRILL

By Len Garner, Head Boys Coach,
North Gwinnett High School, Suwanee, Ga.

Here's a competitive, hard-nosed rebounding drill that teaches your players to be aggressive when fighting for rebounds. Divide your squad into three equal teams. A coach stands just inside the free-throw line, while the three teams each form a line — one line at each elbow and one line down middle at the foul line, **DIAGRAM 1:** *"Banger" Drill.* The first player in each line steps into the paint. The coach tosses the ball off the rim and the three players battle for the ball. The goal for each player is to grab the rebound and put it back up and in for the score.

The rebounder is not allowed to bring the ball down below the chin-

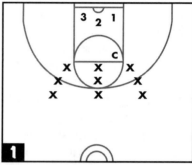

level, dribble or let the ball be knocked loose.

If the player scores, he or she goes to the end of his or her team's line and the next player steps in. Players must score to get out of the pit. The first team to have each player on their team score, wins!

8-SPOT SHOOTING DRILL

By Len Garner, Head Boys Coach,
North Gwinnett High School, Suwanee, Ga.

Here's a simple yet effective shooting drill that gets your players lot of jump shot repetitions. Place four players at each basket in your gym: a rebounder, a shooter and two passers.

DIAGRAM 1: *8-Spot Shooting Drill.* On the coach's signal, the shooter is to take jump shots from each of the 8 spots as shown in the Diagram. The shooter's goal is to make shots from at least 6 of the 8 spots in 21 seconds.

A coach or manager must be stationed at each basket where the drill is taking place and must monitor how the shooter catches the ball, the shooting release, footwork, how he or

she sets up hand targets for the passer and how the player is reacting under the time-limit pressure. The coach or manager calls out the time at 7-second intervals and then counts down the last 7 seconds out loud.

FOOTWORK, CONDITIONING DRILLS

*By Wayne Walters, Former Head Mens Coach,
Thaddeus Stevens College, Lancaster, Pa.*

Basketball is a game of stop-and-go and change-of-direction movements. A player must learn to stop before moving on to another action, otherwise he or she might get called for a travel, charge or commit unnecessary fouls which hurt your individual and team performance.

Most young players are unable to stop while maintaining proper balance before performing another action. A proper jump stop, is performed with the feet shoulder-width apart, stopping on the balls of the feet and a bend of the legs to absorb and stop momentum.

The following are a series of practice drills in which the players will be forced to work on skills such as jump stopping, pivoting, reverse pivoting and changing direction — all while maintaining proper balance.

These drills may seem relatively simple, but for them to be effective, the coach must closely monitor the footwork and stop the drill to make any corrections that need to be made. Once your players master these drills, you'll be amazed at how much it improves their overall skill level.

DIAGRAM 1: *Run-And-Stop Drill.* On

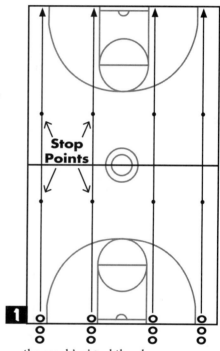

the coach's signal the players run downcourt and come to a proper jump-stop on the coach's command. the coach then signals for the player to resume running and repeats the commands the entire length of the floor.

DIAGRAM 2: *Dribble-Stop-And-Pivot Drill.* The player power dribbles hard downcourt and then comes to a proper stop and pivots on the coach's com-

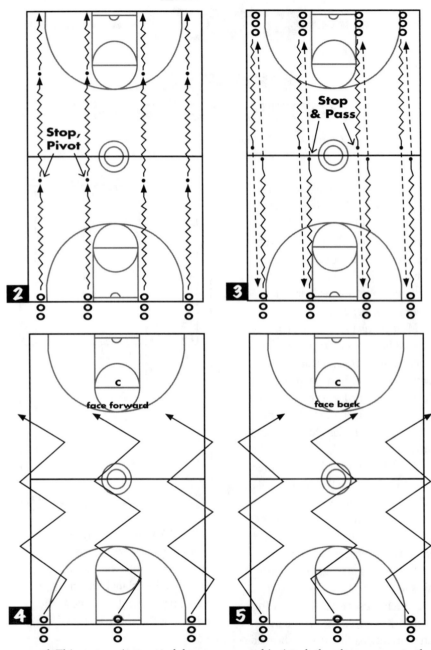

mand. This process is repeated down the entire length of the floor.

DIAGRAM 3: *Dribble-Stop-And-Pass Drill.* Same drill as before, only on the coach's signal, the player passes to the player in line on the opposite end of the floor. Watch for proper jump stops before the pass is made.

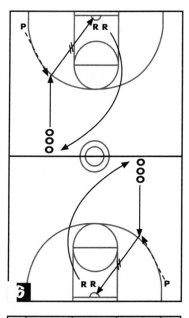

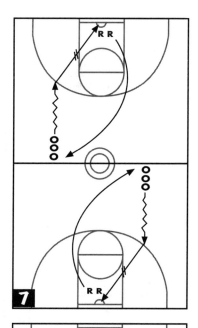

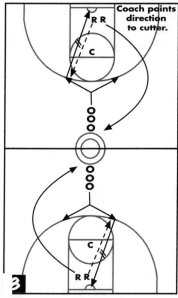

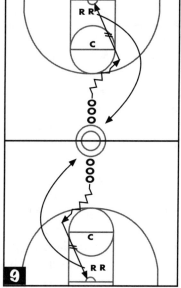

DIAGRAM 4: *"Plant-And-Turn"*
Offense Drill. The player runs, plants
and turns on the coach's signal. Have
them begin by doing the drill while
running, then add repetitions with
"plant and turns" while dribbling.

DIAGRAM 5: *"Plant-And-Turn"*
Defense Drill. Same drill as previously described, only have the defender
execute a change-of-direction on the
coach's signal.

DIAGRAM 6: *"Run-Stop-Catch-And-*

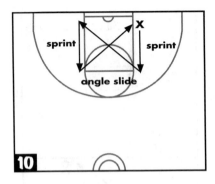

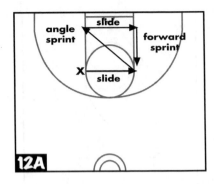

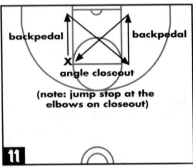

(note: jump stop at the elbows on closeout)

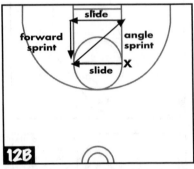

Shoot" Drill. Run this drill with multiple players on both sides of the floor.
DIAGRAM 7: *"Dribble-Stop-Shoot" Drill.* Have two rebounders under the drill and rotate positions. Also run this drill on both sides of the floor.
DIAGRAM 8: *"'Y' Catch-and-Shoot" Drill.* The player runs hard from midcourt and at the top of the 3-point circle, looks for the coach's signal on whether to go left or right. On the coach's signal, the player plants, catches a pass from the rebounder and shoots a jumper. Closely watch the shooter's footwork, hand targets and shooting form while squaring up to the basket.

DIAGRAM 9: *"'Y' Dribble-and-Shoot" Drill.* The same drill as previously described only the player power dribbles, plants and executes a dribble move to either the left or right, depending on which direction the coach signalled.
DIAGRAM 10: *"Running-The-Lane 'X'" Drill.*
DIAGRAM 11: *"Backward 'X' Running" Drill.* Make sure the players execute proper jump stops and close-outs at the elbows.
DIAGRAM 12a, 12b: *"'Z' and 'X' Running" Drill.*

The forward sprints must alternate "Z" slides from the opposite side at the top of the "Z" slide.

"ATTACK-N'-GO" DRILL

By John Lacitignola, Head Girls Coach,
Dansville High School, Dansville, N.Y.

The "Attack N' Go" is a continuous, half-court, all-purpose drill that develops defensive and offensive skills simultaneously. Your team should run it as either a warmup to begin practice or as the first drill in a daily defensive progression series.

Offensively, "Attack N' Go" works on practicing first step moves, passing under pressure, the give-and-go, baseline drives, squaring up and power layups.

Defensively, it works on closing out, sliding to protect the baseline and trapping.

This is a very active drill that involves constant movement and will keep player waiting to a minimum.

player at each elbow and a line of players just below the jump ball circle (outside line).

The drill begins as 5 cuts right, stopping at the wing area just above the 3-point arc. 1 passes the ball to 5 and closes out hard. 5 does not move until 1 is up close playing defense. Stress that the defender must be very active with waving hands and proper defensive stance.

Once 1 has closed out on 5, 2 passes out to 6 on the other side and everything repeats.

DIAGRAM 2: 5 makes a quick move toward the basket using any move to get free. 1 must force 5 to the corner. Once in the corner, 5 picks up the dribble and looks to pass to 4 at the elbow.

At this point, the defender must

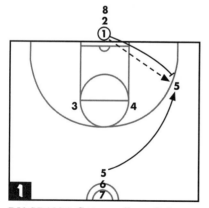

DIAGRAM 1: Set up a line of players under the basket (inside line). The first two have basketballs. Place a

protect the baseline and maintain active hands without reaching in.

Stress that the offensive player make the good pass, faking high and going low, utilizing proper pivot techniques to protect the ball. The quickest way to turn the ball over is to try and throw over the trap.

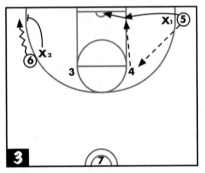

DIAGRAM 3: 5 passes to 4 and immediately cuts to the basket looking for a return bounce pass (1 allows 5 the free cut to the basket). 5 receives the pass and comes to a jump-stop, putting up a power layup.

Stress that the cutter should present the inside hand as a target and upon receiving the pass should square up and go up strong. 5s get their own

rebound and hand-off to the next player in the inside line.

Rotation

1, the defender, moves to the elbow. 5, the offensive player, goes to the end of the inside line and 4, who is at the elbow, goes to the end of the outside line (repeat same on the other side).

Since this drill is continuous, your players must always be hustling and working hard.

Later

Once your players have a feel for the drill, add a coach under the basket with a football blocking pad who randomly defends the shooters.

You want your players to get used to the physical contact that a move of this kind invites. As a result, your players will not shy away during game situations and will concentrate on going up strong.

We have found that after implementing this drill, our players have played a lot harder underneath and, out of habit, look for the return give-and-go pass.

DEFENSIVE TRANSITION DRILLS

By Will Mayer, Head Boys Coach,
Middletown North High School, Middletown, N.J.

Here are two very competitive drills that help improve your player's ability to recover in transition defense.

basket counts for 1 point and any defensive stop or turnover results in minus 2 points for the offensive team. After both teams have played offense for the 3 minutes, the team with the least amount of points runs laps.

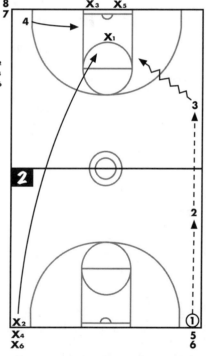

DIAGRAM 1: *"Never-Too-Late" Drill.*
The drill runs for 3 minutes and then offense and defense switch off. Player C inbounds the ball to 1 or 2. X2, starting at the hash mark, gets back on defense, while X1(who's positioned on the opposite foul line) sprints in from behind to provide catch-up help defense in transition. Put a scoring system in place where an offensive

DIAGRAM 2: *2-Player Recovery Drill.*
Using the same time-limits and scoring system as in the previous drill, player 1 begins the drill by passing to 2. 2 passes to 3. Players 3 and 4 attack

X1 in a 2-on-1 situation.

X2 must sprint back as soon as 1 makes his or her pass and tries to provide defensive help in transition. The offense rotates after each possession in the following manner: 5 to 1's spot, 1 to 2's spot, 2 to 3's spot, 3 to the end of 4's line and 4 to the end of 1's line.

BONUS DRILL:
5-ON-THE-LINE TRANSITION DRILL

By Bobby Cremins, Former Head Coach
Georgia Tech University, Atlanta, Ga.

ALMOST EVERY team can push the ball up the floor on the fast break. That makes it even more important for your team to play in transition.

This is an excellent drill you can use everyday to work on transition defense. We call it the 5-On-The-Line Drill.

Line up five offensive players on the baseline. Line up five defenders directly in front of the offense around the dotted free-throw circle. Start the drill by passing the basketball to any of the offensive players.

DIAGRAM 1: Two designated defenders much touch the baseline before running back on defense. This sets up a 5-on-3 fast break the other way.

DIAGRAM 2: The two defenders sprint back and scramble to get back into the play. The defenders must communicate to each other where the open player is and who is going to pick up the open players.

"3-PLUS-1" DRILL

By Len Garner, Head Boys Coach,
North Gwinnett High School, Suwanee, Ga.

Here's an easy-to-run, yet efficient defensive drill that improves your player's knowledge of team defense, rotations and teaches them how to give and receive defensive help.

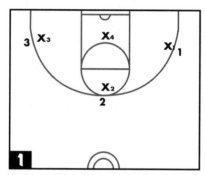

DIAGRAM 1: *3-Plus-1 Drill.* Set up three defensive players along the perimeter, just under the 3-point circle. Place a fourth defender in the middle of the lane (X4). Three offensive players are positioned on the perimeter, outside the 3-point circle and move the ball from side-to-side, looking to penetrate and score.

The defensive players must work on containment, help-side defense and the middle post-player rotation. The player in the middle (X4) must communicate with his or her teammates on defense — alerting them to picks, slide throughs, etc.

Run a predetermined number of offensive possessions or run the drill for a set time limit and then have the defensive perimeter players switch to offense and have a new group of defensive players step in.

"AMBASSADOR"
(6-PLAYER, 2-BALL WEAVE) DRILL

By Bill Martin, Head Girls Coach,
Xenia Christian High School, Xenia, Ohio

This drill is basically two, 3-player weaves interwoven together, utilizing two basketballs simultaneously. It's a challenging drill that demands concentration and good passing skills and can be used as either a full-court or half-court drill.

DIAGRAM 1: *Ambassador Drill.* Start with two balls at the same time in the 3-player weave and have both groups of three running the weave. The two groups of players run the weave, making sure that they pass within their own group and not trip over one another.

If executed properly, the players who make the first pass, should be the ones who make the layup at their respective side of the basket.

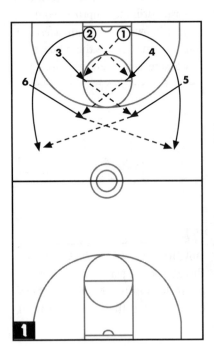

CIRCLE BREAK DRILL

By Steve Pappas, Head Boys Coach,
Deerfield High School, Deerfield, Ill.

This is a great all-purpose drill that incorporates all phases of the game. It can be run with restrictions, but it's an excellent drill for building conditioning and toughness.

How It's Run

Divide your squad into four groups. If possible, each group should have a different colored shirt.

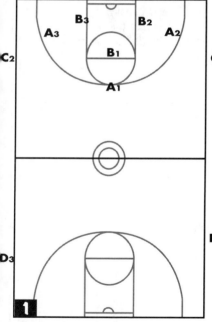

DIAGRAM 1: Team A will be on offense and attacks team B. The two teams play full court and stay on the floor until one team scores. The team that scores must get back on defense while the team waiting under the scoring basket inbounds the ball and attacks.

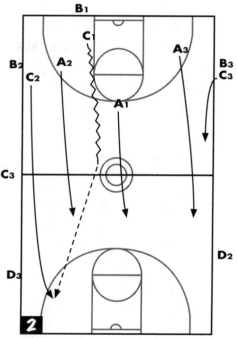

DIAGRAM 2: If team A scores, team B will step off the floor and align at the positions at that basket. Team A will get back on defense and team C steps on the floor on offense.

C1 gets the ball out of the net and bursts up court with a dribble or a pass. As soon as the ball goes in the basket, C2 and C3 have the opportunity to move up the court. Their initial alignment is at the free-throw line extended.

The next team in does not have to take the ball out of bounds, as they can grab the ball coming through the basket and go.

When a team steps off the court, they occupy the positions under the basket and sideline and must be prepared to enter the drill once a goal is scored at their basket.

Keep track of the score and play for a specific time limit. Fouls result in points, with the fouling team stepping off the court.

The Circle Break drill may be run with a "no dribble" restriction. Allow contact to help players toughen-up with the ball. Reward players diving for loose balls and giving extra effort. **DRILL EMPHASIS:** Fast-break principles, getting back on defense, three-on-three and four-on-four motion principles.

BONUS DRILL: THE T.O.T.A.L. DRILL
(3-ON-3 ABSOLUTE LEARNING)

By Wynn Wingate, Basketball Coach,
Belaire High School, Baton Rouge, La.

THIS DRILL ENHANCES:
✔ Defensive skills
✔ Offensive skills
✔ Conditioning
✔ Competitiveness

STEP 1: Separate the team into two equal teams. Use two balls.

STEP 2: Put 15 minutes on the clock (you can vary the time).

STEP 3: Arrange the two teams as in the diagram.

Offensive players 1,2 and 3 attack the defense. The offense can score 2 or 3 points on a made basket and 1 point for a defensive foul. If the offense scores, the defensive trio stays on the court and faces a new trio of offensive players coming down the court. The offensive trio that scored fills the back of the offensive lines.

If the defense holds, all six players run off the court and six new players begin immediately.

STEP 4: At the 7:30 mark (half way through the drill), the offense and defense switch roles. The score at halftime is usually in favor of the team that had the ball first. By the end of the drill the score is usually close.

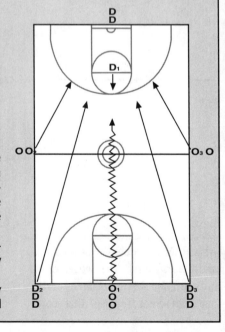

PERFECT PRACTICE DRILLS

WARMUP DRILLS

By Phil Martelli, Head Mens Coach,
St. Joseph's University, Philadelphia, Pa.

OUR TEAM STARTS every practice with a team drill that serves as a great warmup routine. During each warmup drill, time your players and give them a goal to attain. Once your players meet the time and goal, have them move on to the next drill.

After a healthy set of warmup drills, your practices will be crisp, sharp and productive.

Keep Players Challenged

Are your drills symmetrical? Do they have a flow that's fresh and challenging?

The first coach that I worked for warmed up the team the same way every day for the first 5 years. We did a drill called "Jack Ramsey," followed by two-line layups and a brief scrimmage. Everyday — the same thing — for 5 years!

Finally, one day I said to the head coach, "Do you think we could run the Jack Ramsey drill to the left side?" And the answer was, "No. Ramsey always did it to the right side."

It's important to mix things up and keep your players thinking and challenged. Communication is one of the skills that players lack, so talk to the oldest players before warmups and say, "Be ready, we're going to switch directions in the drill at the 2-minute mark, so let your teammates know!"

JACK RAMSEY DRILL

We've named the following drill after Hall of Fame coach Jack Ramsey, who won a NBA title as the head coach of the Portland Trailblazers, and was a coach at St. Joseph's and is currently a NBA expert on ESPN. In the St. Joe's gym, this drill has been done forever.

It's a simple, effective warmup drill and can be completed in 4 minutes. It's also a great way to identify if your players are ready to practice.

DIAGRAM 1: *Jack Ramsey Drill.* Form two lines of players with a ball in each line. Coaches or team managers catch and pass. The player passes the ball to the C/M and runs on a dead sprint toward that C/M. As the player runs by the C/M, the C/M flips the ball back to the player. As soon as they secure the ball, without a dribble, they pass ahead to the next C/M.

The C/M hits the sprinting player with a bounce pass and the player shoots a layup. The next player in line takes the ball out of the net and goes the other way passing to the C/M on the other side. This action is repeated for 4 minutes.

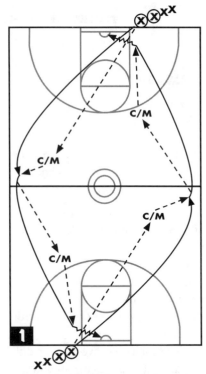

After the 2-minute mark, have the players switch directions, so they're going toward the left side. The C/M moves to the same spot on the opposite side of the floor. Have one coach or team manager who isn't involved in the drill keep track of makes and misses.

Once your players get good at this drill, your team can get well over 100 layups in 4 minutes if you use four balls. Set 100 made layups as the ultimate goal. Initially, set a goal of 90 and they can work their way up.

If missed layups are a problem, add a stipulation that only two to four misses are allowed. We turn on the scoreboard and start it at 4 minutes and post the running tally of made layups on the board. Your players will watch the scoreboard, hustle and cheer each other on.

CELTIC DRILL

The Celtic drill is another four-ball drill with two lines of players positioned off to the side at the foul-line extended. Have a coach or player in the lane as a rebounder.

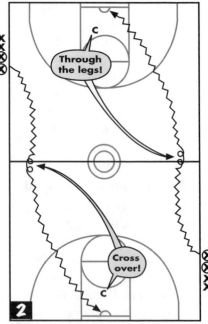

DIAGRAM 2: *Celtic Drill.* The first two players in each line start with a ball. The player at the beginning of the line speed dribbles toward the basket at the other end of the court. When he or she reaches half-court, the coach calls out a dribble move such as "through your legs," "crossover," "stop and go," "behind the back," etc.

After the dribble move is executed, the player continues the speed dribble to the basket for a layup and sprints to the end of the line on that side of the floor. The drill continues for 4 minutes. Switch sides of the floor at the 2-minute mark.

Let Big Players Practice Dribbling

In all your ball-handling drills, encourage your biggest players to handle the ball and run as fast as they can. When a big kid clumsily kicks the ball out of bounds, encourage him or her to go get it and to do the drill again.

If you don't allow that big player to handle the ball in practice in a non-threatening position, do you know what's going to happen when an opponent presses you in a game? That big kid is going to get the ball and he or she is going handle it like it's going to explode.

All you need is for him or her to take two dribbles and cross half-court to break the press, but that player can't because he or she has never dribbled the ball. That's not the player's fault. It's our fault as coaches for not designing drills that allow big players to handle the ball.

VANDERBILT

This drill is a variation of the Jack Ramsey and Celtic drills. If you're having problems with your team's ability to run the floor, this is a great drill.

DIAGRAM 3: *Vanderbilt Drill.* Using four balls and two lines of players, the first player in each line speed dribbles to half court. At half court, the player passes the ball ahead to a coach who's positioned at the 3-point line and the player continues to streak toward the

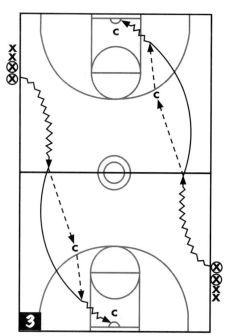

basket. The coach throws the player a bounce pass and the player catches it in stride, lays it in and runs to the end of the closest line. Another coach rebounds the ball and passes it to the first player in the near line.

STANFORD

Our teams have had a lot of problems over the years outletting the basketball. Players were always throwing slow outlet passes and it was a problem that I didn't have an answer for. This weakness became very apparent one year in a game that we lost to Stanford. I noticed that the Stanford players were really crisp with their outlet passes and they killed us in transition. So we call this drill Stanford.

DIAGRAM 4: *Stanford.* The players form one line at one end of the floor. Start one player wide (X1) and station

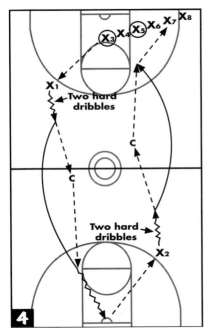

4

another player in the outlet position on the other end of the floor (X2). Two coaches or team managers line up near center court on opposites sides.

The first player in line (X3) does a layup, grabs his or her own rebound and throws an outlet pass to X1. X1 takes two hard dribbles and passes to the coach near half court. X1 sprints down court and receives a pass near the elbow and drives for a layup. After making the layup, X1 gets his or her own rebound and throws an outlet pass to X2, who begins the same action going the other way. After making the outlet pass, X1 takes X2's place as the outlet receiver.

UMASS

If your team didn't play well the night before or didn't play as hard as you'd like them to play, this drill gets

their attention the next day at practice. We call it U Mass because back when John Calipari was in our league and coached at the University of Massachusetts, this is how his team warmed up.

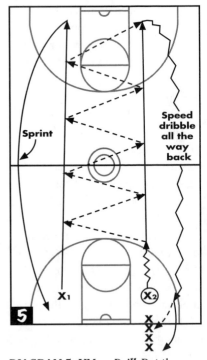

5

DIAGRAM 5: *UMass Drill.* Put the whole team in one line facing in the same direction. The first player in line (X1) walks to the other side of the lane, and with the next person in line (X2), begins to pass the ball back and forth all the way down the court. The player that has the ball once they get to the other side, must speed dribble back on four dribbles, while the other player sprints back. Both players get back into line and the next two players go.

Whether you have 10, 12, 14 or 16 players, this drill gets your players working up a sweat. This is a very difficult drill and is fabulous for conditioning, passing and catching.

PITINO

It's a good idea to periodically mix up your ball-handling drills. Repeating the same drills over and over becomes stagnant and boring for your players and they won't get a lot out of them. One of the ball-handling drills that we use most is called Pitino. DIAGRAM 6: *Pitino Drill.* Split your team into two groups and have each group line up on opposite sides of the court. Set up chairs surrounding the perimeter of the 3-point circle. Each player has his or her own ball.

Station a coach on each side of the floor. One by one, each player begins dribbling around the chairs in the sequence shown. At each chair, the coach calls out a specific dribble move such as "right-to-left crossover." The player executes the required move, drives in for a layup, gets the ball as it comes through the net and begins dribbling toward the next chair. As he or she completes the initial layup, the next player in line begins dribbling and does the same dribble move at

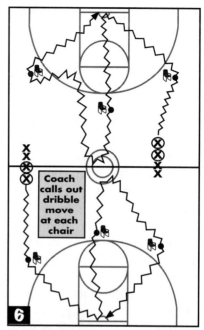

the first chair. We'll actually say at times, "Follow the leader, just follow the leader." The players dribble around all three chairs, finish off with a second layup and sprint back in line.

Do this drill at a good pace for up to 6 minutes. Even though there's constant action in this drill, since it's being done in a half-court setting, it's a good drill to run if you're trying to save your players' legs.

11-Player Break

By Brian C. Laffin, Head Coach,
Poughkeepsie High School, Poughkeepsie, N.Y.

We use this drill each day in practice for 5 to 8 minutes. It's good for both the offensive and defensive improvement of your team. On offense, this drill improves offensive transition, finishing on breaks, communication and works on transition at game-like speed.

Defensively, this drill helps your defenders become more aggressive, gets them into the habit of communicating, gives them work on outnumbered 3-on-2 transition situations and teaches them to force an offense to make an extra pass and/or take a low-percentage jump shot.

OFFENSIVE RULES:

1. Players on the outlet lines must call "outlet."
2. The ball must be centered by a strong dribble after the outlet pass.
3. Players must use a bounce pass when making an across the lane pass.
4. The player in the middle should slide over to the ball-side elbow after making a pass to the wing.
5. All players must have their hands ready to catch any pass at any time.
6. The middle can not go below the foul line.
7. The ball must outlet to the wing on the ball-side.

DEFENSIVE RULES:

1. The defensive players cannot go above the 3-point line.
2. The bottom defender must defend the first pass.
3. The top defender must drop into the lane after the first pass.
4. All defenders must call out "Shot!" on any jump-shot attempt.

RULES AFTER ANY SHOT ATTEMPT:

1. After the shot, it becomes every player for himself or herself.
2. Everyone has the opportunity to rebound the basketball.
3. No one stops until the possession is secure.
4. Defensive and offensive players all compete for the basketball.
5. The player who comes up with the possession, looks to outlet and fill the lane going the other way.
6. The player that gets the rebound or ball coming through the hoop, fills the lane going the other way.

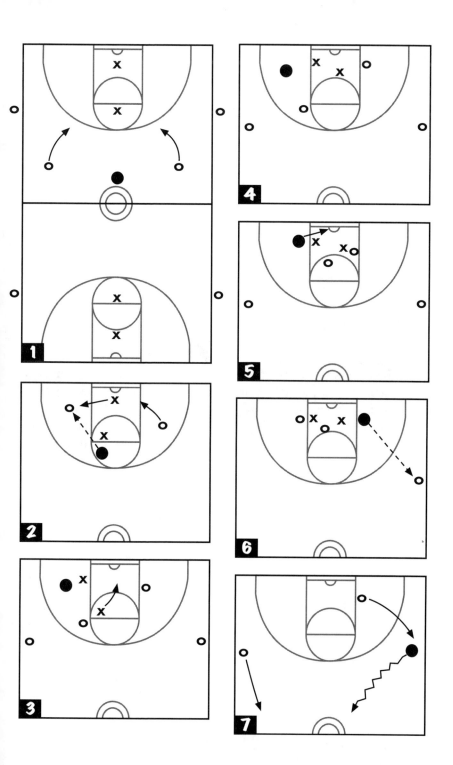

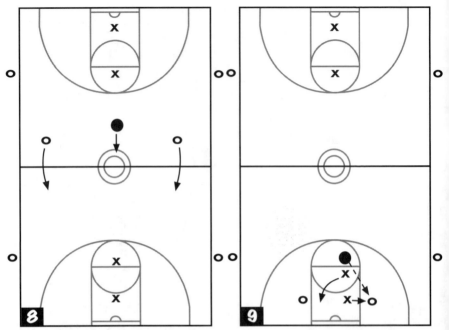

Use the scoreboard clock when running this drill and set it for 8 minutes. The offense's score should be placed on the "Home" portion of the clock and the defense's on the "Visitor" side.

The offense gets 1 point for each make and the defense gets a point for causing a miss or creating a turnover. Have a coach or team manager keep track of all unforced errors and the players must run a sprint for each unforced error. (We also make the players run a sprint each time they are not being competitive.)

CURLS AND FLARES DRILL

By Jason Graves, Head Boys Coach,
Ritenour High School, St. Louis, Mo.

This is a great drill for teaching your players how to read screens. Have a coach positioned at each mid-post area and have three lines of players, one at the top of the key and one in each baseline corner.

"Flare"

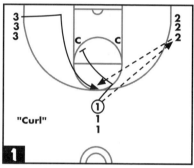

"Curl"

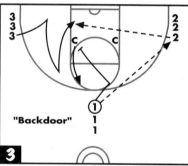

"Backdoor"

DIAGRAM 1: *Curl*. 1 passes to 2 and screens the coach away from the pass. Player 3 breaks from the weak-side corner and curls off the screen and comes over the top to receive the pass.

DIAGRAM 2: *Flare*. If the coach tries to jump under the screen, the player away from the pass uses a flare cut to pop open on the weak side.

DIAGRAM 3: *Backdoor*. If the coach tries to cheat through the player's screen, the backside player, reads the defense (the coach), and cuts back-door for a pass and layup opportunity.

The screener goes to the line closest to where they screened, the initial pass receiver goes to the shooter's line and the shooter goes to the top of the key line.

TEAM SHOOTING DRILL

By Marty Gaughan, Head Boys Coach,
Benet Academy, Lisle, Ill.

Here's a drill that can be used as a pre-game drill or used at two baskets during practice. It can also be a very competitive drill if you keep score and reward the player who makes the most shots in a predetermined amount of time.

This drill serves as a shooting drill that stresses footwork, passing, rebounding and offers a wide variety of different types of shots.

Form your team into two lines, one line is a shooting line, while the other line serves as a passing and rebounding line. Use 4 basketballs and run the drill continuously.

Set up 10 shooting stations as shown in the following three diagrams.

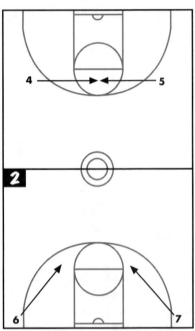

DIAGRAM 2: *Shooting Stations (4 to 7).* 4. Shooting off the cut (across the lane from the right side. 5. Shooting off the cut (across the lane from the left side). 6. Shooting off the cut (from the baseline to the wing on the left side). 7. Shooting off the cut (from the baseline to the wing on the right side).

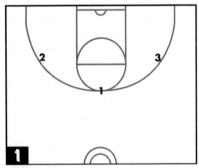

DIAGRAM 1: *Shooting Stations (1 to 3).* 1. Spot-up middle jumper (15 to 17 feet) 2. Spot-up jumper from the right wing (15 to 17 feet) 3. Spot-up jumper from the left wing.

DIAGRAM 3: *Shooting Stations (8 to 10).* 8. Shooting off the fade (from the right side). 9. Shooting off the fade (from the left side). 10. Shooting off the dribble (both right and left sides).

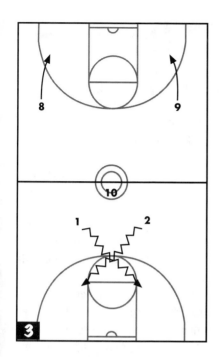

In each of the first 9 stations, have your shooters go to the passing and rebounding line and have the passer go to the shooting line. In the last station, have them form two lines at the top of the key and then shoot off the dribble.

Have your team work on this drill for either a certain number of shots-per-station or to shoot for a certain amount of time from each spot. Deduct points in the drill if a missed shot hits the floor. This forces your players to follow their shots, read the carom off misses and rebound aggressively.

AGGRESSIVE FAST-BREAK DRILL

By Annette Wiles, Head Womens Coach,
Fort Hays State University, Hays, Kan.

We are a team that loves to attack on turnovers, rebounds and made baskets. A sideline fast break that involves passing is the most effective way to attack a retreating defense whether it is a zone or man. Here is an outstanding drill that teaches your players how to run an aggressive fast break.

Running The Drill

In order to run, your players must first establish the defensive rebound and make a proper pivot on the outside foot.

Outlet players are expected to come back to the ball by taking at least two steps and yelling "outlet, outlet" to the rebounder.

Upon receiving the pass, the outlet player must square up in triple-threat position and make the sideline pass up the court to the next outlet player.

The next player must turn and put the ball in the outside hand, with the off arm up and attack the corner or middle of the court for an entry bounce pass to a low-post player who has established good post-up position.

Continuing The Drill

As the low-post player is making the low-post shot, the next rebounder is tossing another ball off the backboard and starting the drill all over again. Each person moves to the next

open position by rotating clockwise.

Repetition of this drill will prepare your players to instinctively run an aggressive fast break. They will automatically know where to go on the floor and what kind of passes they will need to make.

Make sure that the rebounder is practicing proper rebounding technique (boxing out, securing the ball with two hands, elbows high, and proper pivot on the outlet pass) at all times.

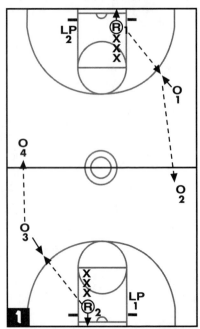

DIAGRAM 1: R1 and R2 each have a ball. At the whistle, each player begins

the drill by throwing the ball off the backboard, secures the rebound and pivots to throw the outlet pass to O1 and O3.

O1 and O3 must come back to the ball and yell "Outlet, outlet!" O1 and O3 pass to O2 and O4.

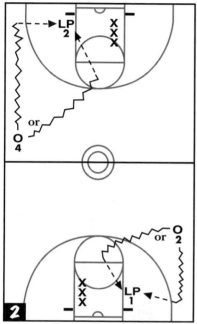

DIAGRAM 2: O2 and O4 attack the corner or make a change of direction dribble to the middle of the court for an entry pass to LP1 and LP2.

LP1 and LP2 must use any one of a variety of post moves (front turn, drop step, hook shot or counter move) and finish by making the basket.

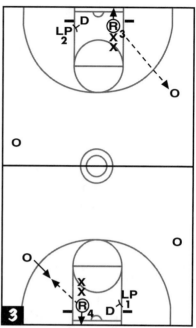

DIAGRAM 3: As an option, you may use a defender to guard your low-post players. Players rotate clockwise. Once they become good at this, add a third and fourth basketball to the drill. This will ensure that the action is fast and that a lot of players get involved.

TOUGHNESS DRILLS

By June Daugherty, Head Womens Coach,
University of Washington, Seattle, Wash.

Hustle and toughness for your team can be improved through hard work in practice and a consistent emphasis by the coaching staff on what it takes to be a mentally and physically tough player. The following drills can help you build a tough team that's ready for battle on game days.

Team Toughness Drills

❖ **RIP DRILL.** To begin the drill, have a coach or manager standing at the elbow. Players form a single-file line from half court. Each player, one by one, makes a pass to the coach, then runs to ball and rips the ball from the coach's hands. After the player has secured the ball, the player makes a power move to the basket and stays on baseline.

❖ **ROLL DRILL.** After all the players have performed the Rip drill, the coach or manager turns around to face the players on the baseline. The player makes a pass to the coach and the coach rolls the ball out along the baseline. The player has to run out to the ball, pick it up, then make a power layup to the basket.

In both the Rip and Roll drills, get your players in the habit of calling the coach's name with each pass. These drills are also great when used with blocking pads or shields. Have addi-tional coaches or managers standing in the key to hit and bump the players as they make their power moves to the basket on rips and rolls.

❖ **90 SECOND THREE'S.** Players partner into groups of two, while a coach or manager keeps track of the time. There are five spots on the floor. Players choose any spots on the floor they wish. Player 1 has to hit three consecutive 3-pointers before he or she can move to the next spot, while player 2 rebounds. The goal is to see how many of the five spots the player can clear before the 90-second time limit expires. Players then switch positions after the first 90 seconds.

Besides shooting, this is also a rebounding drill. The rebounding player should be going up hard for rebounds and making good outlet passes.

❖ **WEAVE SHOOTING.** Players form three lines at half court with the ball in the middle. Players do a three-player weave and after the second pass, the shooter shoots (our team usually takes all 3-point shots in this drill, but depending on your personnel, it may vary for you). The other two players become rebounders and crash the boards hard, trying to secure the rebound before the ball hits the ground.

Don't allow the rebounders to camp out underneath the basket! If the shot is missed, the rebounder puts it back up or can pass it to the second rebounder if he or she has a better, closer shot.

If the ball hits the ground or the offensive rebounder misses the put back, the score resets and those three players run to the end of the line. Managers keep track of points with 3-point shots being worth three points, 2-point shots are worth two and put backs are worth 1 point. Put 3 minutes on the clock for this drill and set up varying goals. After the ball hits the ground a few times and that group's score resets, you'll find that players naturally begin to get on each other. This is a great shooting, rebounding and focus drill!

❖ **SKIP "O" SHOOTING.** Players line up in three lines at half court, with guards and wings on the outside lines and post players in the middle. The ball starts in one of the outside lines. The first pass can go to either the middle or skipped to the opposite wing, where that player shoots a 3-pointer. When the shot is taken, the other two players must crash the boards and put back the offensive rebound. If the ball hits the ground, the score is reset. Use the same scoring system as in the previous drill and put 3 minutes on the clock.

❖ **BOUNCE DRILL.** This is a two-player drill. Player 1 is positioned outside the key midway to the free-throw line to begin. Have either player 2 or a coach bounce the ball hard, so that it goes above the head of 1. After the ball

hits the floor on the initial bounce, 1 may react to the ball. 1 grabs the ball out of the air, simulating a rebound, squares up to the basket and makes a step-through move and scores.

1 may not dribble and the move has to be made on either the right or left side of the basket, not down the middle. Repeat this drill five times on each side and finish with two free throws. If 1 misses a shot, the drill starts over.

❖ **3-ON-0 REBOUND DRILL.** Have a coach or manager on both sides of the basket, outside the key and three players in the middle of the key to begin. A coach throws the ball off the backboard and the three players in the key battle for the rebound and offensive basket. There's no dribbling and anything goes. The first player to make three baskets wins. Emphasize boxing out after the shot on defense and going hard to the offensive glass and following shot on offense.

❖ **CHARGE DRILL.** Partners start on baseline under the basket opposite one another. Player 1 rolls a ball toward free-throw line. Player 1 runs out to get the ball and begins to dribble toward the basket. Player 2 steps in and takes a charge.

❖ **LOOSE-BALL DRILL.** Partners start on baseline under the basket opposite one another. Player 1 rolls the ball out toward the free-throw line. Player 2 dives on the floor for the loose ball, secures it and makes a pass to 1 while still lying on the ground. 1 scores the basket. Repeat, switch or alternate each time.

"40 Game" & "Cutthroat" Drills

By Joe Pitt, Head Boys Coach,
Union High School, Union S.C.

Here are two drill games that are challenging, yet fun for your players.

40 Game

❖ **"40 GAME."** Have your team play 5-on-5 half court and award a point for every pass that's successfully completed, 10 points for a layup and 5 points for any offensive rebound. The first team to 40 points wins.

This is a great drill to teach moving without the ball, passing, offensive rebounds and shot selection. Defensively, it stresses team play and boxing out, as you have to get a stop to to get the ball back and score.

Cutthroat

❖ **"CUTTHROAT."** This is a great drill to develop the overall intensity of your players, team and individual defense and shot-selection tendencies. Divide your squad into three teams and play 4-on-4, with each team getting five possessions. You can only score points in the following manner:
1. A defensive stop (worth 1 point).
2. Taking a charge (worth 2 points).
3. Offensive basket (worth 1 point).
4. Offensive rebounds (worth 1 point).

At the end of the five possessions per team, total each team's score. The team with the fewest points, runs the most laps. The second-place teams runs some laps and the winning team doesn't run at all.

5-PLAYER DRILL

By Tammy Hedspeth, Basketball Coach,
St. Gertrude High School, Richmond, Va

Coaches are always on the lookout for drills that incorporate several skills at once so that practice time is used more efficiently.

After several adjustments, we've created one that works on boxing out, rebounding, outlet passing, passing, shooting, and conditioning all at once.

Five players are needed as well as two balls and one basket. You can run this drill at multiple baskets at one time with groups of five players. The five players are assigned roles:

❖ One shooter.

❖ Two rebounders.

❖ One outlet receiver/passer.

❖ One passer.

DIAGRAM 1: Begin with the shooter taking a shot, immediately sprinting to the baseline and back to receive the 2nd ball from the passer for the next shot.

Meanwhile, both rebounders work

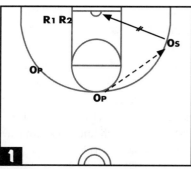

for position, rebound the ball and hit the outlet player. The outlet player hits the passer and the passer hits the shooter. The shooter takes 25 shots.

After 25 shots, each player rotates clockwise to a different position. Run this drill until each player takes 25 shots. Add competition by making the rebounder who gets the fewest rebounds run five sprints. Vary where the shot is being taken and have your outlet player move around freely, which forces the rebounders to pay attention to their outlet passes.

"INNER-CITY" DRILL

By Greg Williamson, Head Boys Coach,
Garden City High School, Garden City, Mich.

This is a very competitive drill that challenges the offensive players by limiting the amount of dribbling that they can do. Divide your squad into three teams (A, B and C) and have them line up in single-file lines at one basket as shown in the diagram. The first player in each line steps into play and A has a basketball.

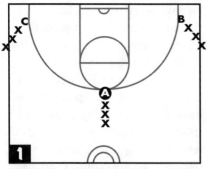

DIAGRAM 1: The first player in line A shoots a 3-pointer. The ball is "live" and in play, regardless of whether the

shot is a make or miss (on a make the 3-points do not count). The game then becomes 1-on-1-on-1 with the player who grabbed the rebound being the one on offense.

The team of the player who scores receives a point and then that team gets to move to the top of the 3-point arc to take a shot and resume the game. The next player in each line steps into play and the players who were on the court rotate to the end of their respective lines.

The first team to 4 points wins (this will give at least 12 players a chance to have battled it out). We'll often play more than one game and position the lines in different areas of the court, so that — on the 3-point shot — the players have to run toward the basket from different angles.

3-On-2 Full-Court Drill

By Dave Witzig, Head Boys Coach,
Normal Community High School, Normal, Ill.

Coached are always searching for new and exciting drills that will get their players warmed up and ready to go. The following 3-on-2 full-court drill works on several skills simultaneously and is one we use daily within the first 15 minutes of practice.

This multi-purpose drill is effective because it teaches players to:

❖ Take advantage of a quick 3-on-2 situation.

❖ Screen and cut during 3-on-3 play.

❖ Break trapping presses by cutting into the middle of the floor.

❖ Trap defensively while not committing fouls.

❖ Protect the basket in fast-break situations.

How The 3-On-2 Drill Works

Divide your squad into two equal teams (teams A and B as shown in the diagram). One team should be positioned on a sideline, while the other team lines up downcourt on the opposite sideline.

DIAGRAM: 3-On-2 Full-Court Drill. Three offensive players from Team A line up at halfcourt, with the middle player holding a ball. On the coach's whistle, Team A attempts to score on Team B in a 3-on-2 attacking situation. Team B starts with two players defensively, one

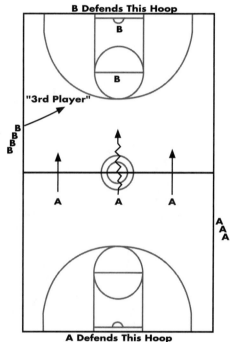

B Defends This Hoop

"3rd Player"

A Defends This Hoop

at the foul line and the other in the lane, positioned in front of the basket.

A third defender for Team B stands on the sideline and waits until the coach calls "Third player in!" At that moment, the third member of Team B sprints in to offer defensive help, turning the drill into a 3-on-3 contest.

If the offense (Team A) scores, they immediately full-court press and look to double-team everything they can in the backcourt. Meanwhile, two new defenders for Team A set up in the front court (one defender at the foul line and the other in front of the basket) and prepare to defend the basket.

Team B is now on offense and tries to break Team A's full-court press. If Team A steals the ball, they try to score again on their end. If Team B breaks the press and the ball passes halfcourt, the pressing defenders on Team A sprint off the court and return to their sideline.

Team B, after breaking the press, takes the ball downcourt and attacks Team A's two back defenders in a 3-on-2 situation. The third Team A defender sprints in to provide defensive help on the coach's call of "Third player in!"

Games are played to 8 points with the losing team doing pushups or sprints. This drill is fast paced, aggressive and your players will love it!

BONUS DRILL:
WARM-UP DRILL GETS YOUR PRACTICES ROLLING

By Bill Salyers, Program Director And Head Coach,
The Kingdom Crusaders AAU, Dayton, Ohio

THIS IS ONE drill that I've found that conditions the players, allows them to be creative, allows the coach to view progress, teaches individual fundamentals and is fun.

Each player has a ball and is lined up at half court. The drill consists of repetitions of three types of shots from both the right and left sides of the court.

✗ Layups. ✗ Jump stop - shot in the paint. ✗ Jump shots.

Before the first player starts to the basket, the coach indicates the type of dribble that the player should use. For instance, the first round might be a speed dribble. The next might be a crossover, behind-the-back, stutter, inside-out or between-the-legs dribble. Finally, they must combine two moves of their choice as they make their way to the basket.

For example, the coach might say "Speed dribble." Each player in line would use a speed dribble to attack the basket for a layup, get their own rebound and go to half court on the other side of the floor.

As soon as the last person in line goes from the right side, the first person in line on the other side repeats the speed dribble layup, but this time from the left side and returns to half court on the right side.

Once the last person from the left side has shot his or her initial layup, the first person goes again, only this time the player uses a speed dribble and executes a jump-stop shot in the paint. On the shot, they must shoot a bank shot after a head-and-ball fake, get their own rebound and move to the other side of the floor.

Once they've completed one rotation with all three types of shots, they're ready to start over with a different dribble approach. The coach designates the next move. No matter the dribble move, they must repeat the same series of 6 shots. The coach watches closely and removes any player from the line that needs special attention.

Give awards to the player that makes the most attempted shots. While a player is in line waiting to go, require them to work on hand strength and coordination drills with the ball.

"4-On-3 Scramble" & "4-On-3 Contest" Drills

By Will Mayer, Head Boys Coach,
Middletown North High School, Middletown, N.J.

Here are two drill games that help improve your players on both offensive and defensive rebounding. They also stress defense, ball movement, cutting, passing, 3-point shooting and penetration to the basket.

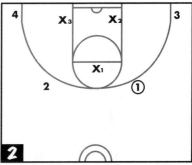

DIAGRAM 2: *4-On-3 Contest Drill.* Play 4-on-3 just as in the previous drill, except that this time, offensive players are allowed only 1 dribble every time they catch a pass and they must be behind the 3-point line to receive a pass. The offense must shoot within 24 seconds. On any shot attempt, the offensive players crash the boards. However, because it's 4-on-3, one offensive player will not be boxed-out by a defender — and that player is not allowed to get the rebound. If the offense gets the offensive rebound, it counts as a score.

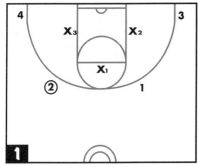

DIAGRAM 1: *4-On-3 Scramble Drill.* In this drill three defenders (X1, X2 and X3) take on four offensive players. The offensive players begin on the perimeter and can only score by making layups or shots in the paint. Each pass the defense forces the offense to make counts as a point for the defense.

Play three to five possessions at a time and then switch defense to offense (the coach keeps one player on offense to still make it a 4-on-3 game). The team with the least amount of points at the end of the drill, runs laps.

The defense must get 2 or 3 stops in a row (depending on what the coach wants) to switch to offense. One player (selected by the coach) stays on offense to keep the drill 4-on-3. Run this drill for a predetermined time limit. The team with the least amount of points at the end of the drill, runs laps.

HELP-AND-RECOVER DRILL

By Andy Vanfossan, Head Boys Coach,
Washington High School, Cherokee, Iowa

This drill encourages your offensive players to make good entry passes into the post and stresses ball movement. On defense, this drill teaches defenders to quickly collapse and attack on-the-ball.

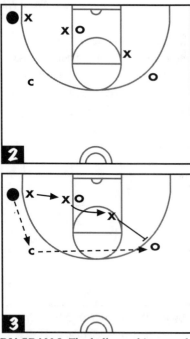

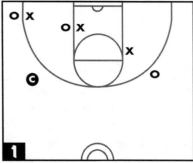

DIAGRAM 1: Set up the drill so that it's 3-on-3 with a tight man-to-man defense. Set up an offensive player on the left low block, one in the left corner and one wide to the right-side wing area. A coach holds a basketball and is on top on the left side.

DIAGRAM 2: The coach begins play by passing the ball into the corner. As the ball is passed into the corner, the corner player's defender should attack and close-out quickly (yet stay under control and not foul). the post defender should fight for position and front the post player on the ball-side block. The backside wing collapses down into the lane to take away any lob passes.

DIAGRAM 3: The ball can skip passed cross-court or be passed back to the coach for quick ball reversals. As the ball is reversed, the help defense must jump to the ball and close-out quickly. The post defender fights to re-establish front-position in the lane as the offensive post player rolls to the ball-side block. The corner defender collapses for help and for blocking out.

The offense quickly moves the ball around the perimeter (with help from the coach) and looks for a good scoring opportunity with either an open jump shot or entry pass into the post.

"CAROLINA" FAST-BREAK DRILL

By Greg Miller, Head Boys Coach,
Armstrong High School, Minneapolis, Minn.

Here's a terrific conditioning and transition drill that's also commonly referred to as "The Old Dean Smith Drill." Two teams of five set up, along with a coach on each baseline, holding a basketball.

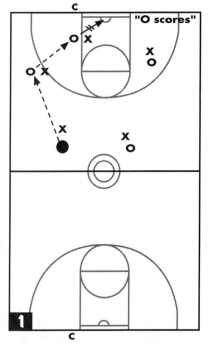

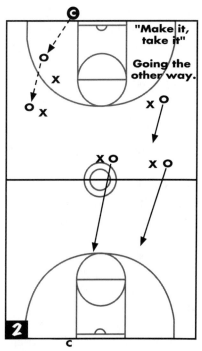

DIAGRAM 1: A jump ball starts a normal game of 5-on-5.

DIAGRAM 2: If a team scores, the coach at that end of the floor throws an outlet pass to the point guard of the team that scored (make-it, take-it) and they run a fast break going the other way downcourt. The outlet must be received inside the 3-point line.

If a team misses a shot, play is continued just as in a normal game and the team that secured the rebound transitions downcourt. To keep the game moving, and turnover or deflection out of bounds results in in an outlet pass to the team who would normally receive it.

Play up to a predetermined score or set time limit. To mix things up, you can occasionally add in a "no-dribbling" rule that emphasizes passing and moving without the ball.

"PURDUE" FULL-COURT DRILL

By Kristy Curry, Head Womens Coach,
Purdue University, West Lafayette, Ind.

Here's a competitive team drill that our players ask to run on almost a daily basis. Run at full speed in game-like conditions, this drill emphasizes passing, catching, communication and finishing layups. It can also serve as an excellent warmup drill.

Position the players on the floor as shown in the diagram prior to starting the drill.

DIAGRAM 1: On the coach's signal, O1 begins the drill by passing to X1. O1 runs hard downcourt, receives a pass back from X1, passes ahead to X2 without dribbling and continues to sprint downcourt, receiving the pass back from X2 after O1 cross the half-court line. O1 then passes ahead to X3, who returns the pass back to O1 in full stride at about the mid-post of the lane line for a layup.

Simultaneously, on the opposite side of the floor, O2 passes to X4. X4 throws a return pass to O2, who throws ahead to X5 at half court. X5 makes a return pass to O2, who passes ahead to X6. X6 returns the pass, hitting O2 in stride for a layup.

Each player grabs the ball as it comes through the net and throws it to the next player waiting in line (X7 and X8 respectively). Once each player in line has made a layup, they rotate down a spot and keep the drill moving. When

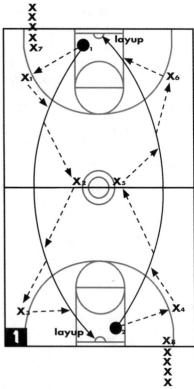

O1 has made layups from both sides, for example, he or she would replace X1, X1 would move down to X2's spot, etc.

The drill continues for a predetermined amount of time. Set goals for this drill (such as a certain number of made layups within a set time limit). If the goals aren't met, the players must perform push-ups. Also build in certain penalties for the number of missed layups, turnovers, etc.

SHOOTING, BALL-HANDLING DRILLS

By Eric Musselman, Former Head Coach,
Golden State Warriors, Oakland, Calif.

The key to any drill is the commitment of the player to go hard at all times — nothing casual. Your players must perform all drills at game speed. A drill's success depends on the player's work ethic.

Keep your drills as competitive as possible for your players. Write down scores and have your players try to beat their previous high. Look for overall improvement from your team every day as the season progresses. A good drill will develop your players mental toughness.

Fast-Break/Turnover Drill

This is a great drill for improving your player's ability to change direction quickly when in transition during a turnover, catch passes on the move and make fast-break layups at full speed.

DIAGRAM 1: *Fast-Break, Turnover Drill.* Player 2 has the ball under the basket and 1 stands anywhere on the

floor. 2 passes to 1, sprints toward him or her and touches the ball.

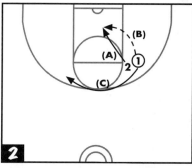

DIAGRAM 2: As soon as 2 touches the ball, he or she immediately turns and sprints back toward the basket. As 2 is sprinting, 1 lobs the ball over 2's head. 2 must gain control of the ball and put in a layup while running at full speed. While 2 is making the layup, 1 moves to another spot on the floor.

DIAGRAM 3: 2 grabs the ball as it comes through the basket, pivots, locates 1, immediately fires a pass

back to him or her, sprints toward 1 and touches the ball.

DIAGRAM 4: After touching the ball, 2 immediately turns and sprints back toward the basket. As 2 is sprinting, 1 lobs the ball just over 2's head. 2 gains control of the ball and puts in a layup while running at full speed. While 2 is making the layup, 1 moves to another spot on the floor.

The drill continues at full speed until 2 makes five layups in a row.

4-Of-5 Shooting Drill

This is a competitive, but fun drill that improves your players mid-range jump shooting.

DIAGRAM 5: *4-Of-5 Shooting Drill.* Set out five pre-determined spots on the floor from 18 feet out going around the basket in an arc. 1 begins from the corner and shoots five shots from 18 feet.

3 rebounds each shot, pivots and makes a crisp outlet pass to 2 who passes back to 1 for another jumper.

1 must make 4-of-5 shots from that spot before he or she can advance to the next spot. If 1 doesn't make the required 4-of-5 shots, then the players rotate and 2 becomes the shooter, 3 the passer and 1 the rebounder.

If a player gets to the next spot, he or she must make 4-of-5 from that spot to advance. If that player fails to get 4-of-5, they must go back one spot.

Players compete to see which player moves the farthest around the horn. Set a time limit or designate the amount of times each player gets to shoot

Explosion Layups

This is a great ball-handling and conditioning drill that forces your players to dribble as fast as they can, while staying under control, exploding to the basket and making strong layups with both hands.

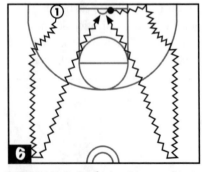

DIAGRAM 6: *Explosion Layups.* Starting on the baseline, 1 dribbles hard to the half-court line with the right hand. When 1 reaches mid-court, he or she makes a change-of-direction move, switches to a left-hand dribble, takes the ball back toward the basket,

explodes to the hoop and finishes with a left-handed layup.

After making the layup, 1 grabs the ball as it's coming through the hoop, takes it to the opposite side of the basket and dribbles hard with the left hand to half-court. At mid-court, he or she makes a change-of-direction move and dribbles hard to the basket with the right hand and finishes with an explosive, right-handed layup.

Shooting Drills

Once your players know how these drill work, allow them to mix up the three types of shots without letting the defenders know which one they will run. This will force your defenders to play hard and teach them how to fight through screens.

DIAGRAM 7: *Getting Open Off Screens.* Players 2 and 3 line up under the basket. 4 sets up on the block. 1, your point guard, handles the ball near the top of the key. 2, while keeping eye contact with 1, fakes left, then tries to run his or her defender off 3's defender and pops to the wing off a screen set by 4. 1 passes to 2 for a quick catch-and-shoot.

DIAGRAM 8: In this drill, 3 tries to turn his or her teammate into the defender in order to free 2, who fades

into the corner. 3 comes over the top of 4's screen. 1 passes to 2 for a catch-and-shoot in the corner.

DIAGRAM 9: Another option off this formation. 2 runs off 3's defender, but this time, instead of breaking off 4's screen, 2 curls around 3 for a quick catch-and-shoot in the lane.

Shooting Over Mt. Mutombo. This drill helps your players learn how to penetrate and shoot over big post players like Dikembe Mutombo. Stress learning how to use the glass and shooting with arch.

DIAGRAM 10: 1 begins on the right elbow, dribbles across the lane and arches the shot high off the glass for a layup.

DIAGRAM 11: 1 begins at the top of the key and dribbles hard down the lane and over the defender. Stress shooting touch arch and body control to avoid getting a charging call.

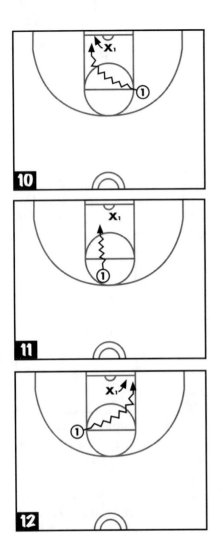

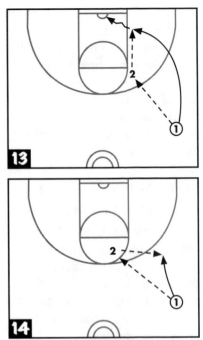

DIAGRAM 14: *Fast-Break 3-Point Shot* Follow the same formation as with the previous drill. 1 passes to 2 and drives hard to the wing, then stops and fades behind the 3-point line. 2 passes back to 1 for the 3-point shot.

DIAGRAM 12: 1 begins on the left elbow, dribbles hard across the lane and shoots high off the glass.

Fast-Break Drills

The following drills help teach your players how to finish off fast breaks and maintain body control.

DIAGRAM 13: *Fast-Break Warm-Up.* 1 passes to 2, makes a basket cut and receives a pass back from 2 just inside the block. 1 finishes the layup without taking a dribble.

DIAGRAM 15: *Fast-Break Crossover Dribble.* 1 passes to 2 and cuts toward the free-throw line extended. 2 passes back to 1. 1 crosses over to the middle of the lane and shoots a pull-up jumper from just inside the foul line.

4-ON-4 DEFENSIVE SHELL DRILL

*By Ron Judson, Head Mens Coach,
Northern Illinois University, DeKalb, Ill.*

Here's a 4-on-4 shell drill we use to build up our defensive tenacity. In the following diagrams, players 1, 2, 3 and 4 are on offense, while A, B, C and D represent the defensive players.

DIAGRAM 1: *Jump To The Ball.* When the ball is passed on the perimeter, the defenders move in what we call "off-the-man and toward-the-cutter" action.

DIAGRAM 2: *Front The Cutter.* An offensive player makes a pass to the wing, he or she makes a ball-side cut. This momentarily empties the post

and C would have to drop down, as B jumps to the ball. As the offensive players move toward the ball, the defenders follow their assigned opponents.

DIAGRAM 3: *Downscreens.* If the ball is reversed and a downscreen is set on the help side, C fights through the screen on the ball side, while B drops down to stay with the screener. Defenders must always "jump to the ball" and close-out when their assigned opponent gets the ball.

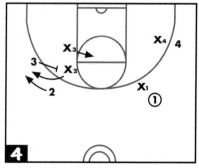

DIAGRAM 4: *Backscreens.* If a backscreen is set on B when the ball is

reversed, B flares over the top of the screen, While C Stays with the screener, hedging toward the ball side.

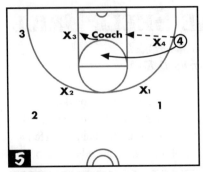

DIAGRAM 5: *Feed-The-Post Shell Drills (A)*. For the Feed-The-Post-Shell Drills, place a coach in the post and do not assign a defender on him or her. This shows movements for a pass into the post and cut to the opposite side of the floor.

DIAGRAM 6: *Feed-The-Post Shell Drills (B)*. Movements for a pass in to the post and screen away.

DIAGRAM 7: *Feed-The-Post Shell Drills (C)*. Movements for a pass in to the post and spot up.

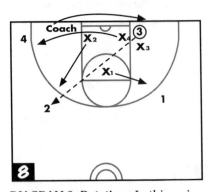

DIAGRAM 8: *Rotations*. In this variation, the coach always moves along the baseline opposite to the side where the ball has been passed. Work on help rotation and close-outs.

"OKLAHOMA" DRILL

By Joe Pitt, Head Boys Coach,
Union High School, Union, S.C.

This is a great shooting drill that also encompasses passing, finishing in transition, shooting, dribbling and conditioning. Set up the 11 players as shown in the diagram — with two players in each corner and three players spaced out evenly along the half-court line.

DIAGRAM 1: *"Oklahoma" Drill.* The player with the ball in the middle begins the drill taking a few hard dribbles and passes to the player streaking to the basket on the right side. That player receives the pass and goes in for a layup. After making the layup, the player gets the ball as it comes through the net and power dribbles down the middle of the floor.

The first passer cuts to the right corner, receives a pass from a player in the right corner and shoots a jump shot. After shooting the jump shot, the shooter follows the shot, retrieves the rebound and goes to the end of the line in the right corner. After making the pass, the passer from the right corner sprints hard downcourt, receives a pass back from the player who is power dribbling down the middle of the floor and makes a layup. The dribbler cuts to the left after making the pass, receives a pass from a player in the near corner and shoots a jump shot. The shooter follows the shot, retrieves the rebound and gets in line the lower right corner.

At the same time all that action is happening, the middle player running on the left side receives a pass from a player in the upper left corner and shoots a jumper. After shooting the jumper, that player follows the shot, retrieves the rebound and goes to the end of the line in the upper left corner. After making the pass, the player from the left corner sprints downcourt, receives a pass from the player in the near corner and shoots a jumper. After shooting the jumper, the shooter follows the shot, retrieves the rebound and goes to the end of the line in the lower left corner.

The player who made the second layup retrieves the ball as it's coming through the net and takes the ball back to the center of the floor. The first two players in each line at the bottom come to the mid-court line on each side of the player with the ball and the drill continues.

Once each player has made a shot from each end of the floor, they will switch to the other side of the floor (either left or right, depending on where they started). This drill goes for a predetermined time limit and you can set goals for made jump shots and layups within a set time limit.

BONUS DRILL: FUN DRILLS TO SHARPEN BALL-HANDLING SKILLS

By Dick Luther, Assistant Mens Coach,
University of Wisconsin-Waukesha, Waukesha, Wis.

WHEN YOU NEED to break up the monotony of practices, but still work on the necessary skills, here are some fun drills.

BIG BALL, SMALL BALL. Have your players do the following three drills using the "Big Ball" and then tennis balls.

1. Have your players do a stationary dribble with a tennis ball in a very low position using both the right and left hand.
2. Dribble in a protective stance.
3. Have your players choose a partner. Using one tennis ball, have them jog the length of the court and bounce pass the tennis ball to each other. This is a great drill to improve a player's hand-eye coordination.

LOOSE-BALL DRILL. Throw the ball and have your players chase it, one at a time. Have a mat for players to land on for safety.

PASSING FOOTBALL GAME. This is a full-court, 4-on-4 drill. Have one team take the ball out of bounds. The other team matches up and defends. Players can only pass and no dribbling is allowed. If the offensive team advances the ball and makes the catch in the defending team's free-throw lane, it's a touchdown for 6 points. If any pass is dropped, the other team takes over at the spot. This drill is great to work on passing and catching, cuts and defense.

BREAK ADVANTAGE DRILL

By Marty Gaughan, Head Boys Coach,
Benet Academy, Lisle, Ill.

This drill is used to create advantages and disadvantages in true break situations and must be run with a great deal of intensity and communication among players. Stress to your players that they must rotate on defense and find the open player on offense.

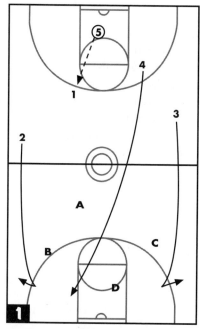

DIAGRAM 1: *5-on-4 Break.* The drill starts by having five offensive players attacking four defensive players in a transition situation. The object for the offensive team is to find the open player, make the extra pass, take care of the

ball and get a great shot. Defensively, the outnumbered defenders work on help-and-recovery techniques, constant helping, communication and rotation.

The possession ends with either a made basket, defensive rebound or turnover. After the possession, two offensive players leave the floor — the initial shooter and last passer.

Important Coaching Note: If there is a turnover, your offensive players must quickly communicate with one another to determine which three players must get back on defense and which two will drop out.

DIAGRAM 2: *4-On-3 Break.* The four defensive players become offensive players and attack the remaining three players in a 4-on-3 transition situation. The same "drop-out rules" apply with the shooter and last passer, leaving the court.

DIAGRAM 3: *3-On-2 Break.* The remaining three defenders become offensive players and attack the last two defenders in a 3-on-2 situation.

After the basket, rebound or turnover, the "drop-out rules" still apply and the remaining players come down one last time in a 2-on-1 situation.

In a 3-on-2 or 2-on-1 transition situation, the mentality of the offensive players is to attack. You want the

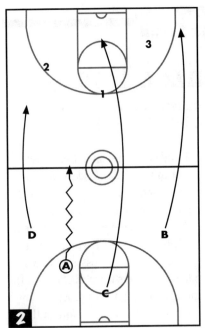

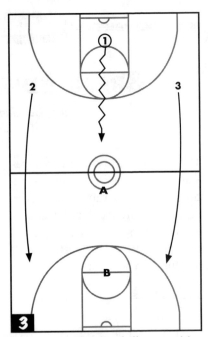

offense to take advantage of the numbers situation and get a shot off early in the possession. (In the 5-on-4 or 4-on-3 situations, the offensive priorities should focus on quick ball movement and getting a great high-percentage shot.)

You can make this drill competitive by having two teams of players (the players decide who sits out first — but all must be rotated in at some point) and keep score. Play for either a set time limit or predetermined number of points.

5-ON-5 FULL-COURT DRILL

By Dick Lemmon, Head Girls Coach,
Barr-Reeve High School, Montgomery, Ind.

Here's a competitive 5-on-5 full-court drill that stresses the importance of offensive and defensive rebounding, fast breaks, pressure defense, press-breaking offense, half-court defense, half-court offense, protecting the basketball and getting a good shot each time down the floor.

Scoring System

With team managers keeping score, give each team three possessions and have them play exclusively man-to-man. Follow this with three possessions by each team, having them play strictly zone defense. Reward the winners and punish the losers with extra conditioning work.

The next phase of the drill begins as a 5-on-5 block-out drill with points being awarded for desired activities. Points are awarded for the following achievements:

❖ 3 points for an offensive rebound.
❖ 2 points for a defensive rebound or steal.
❖ 1 point for any type of basket.
❖ Turnovers are counted as steals for the other team.

Initiating The Drill

This drill can be initiated in a number of ways, depending on what you wish to emphasize during practice.

The coach can pass to an offensive player from the baseline or the coach may pass from mid-court to initiate the drill.

You can also have an offensive player start at three-quarter court either by dribbling or passing to start the offense. The method used usually depends on how satisfied you are with the level of play of certain aspects of your team.

Defensive Rules, Communication

Start with a coach on the baseline. All defensive players must have their feet inside the lane. The coach passes the ball to a stationary offensive player. The defensive players must quickly establish defensive position based on the position of the ball and their offensive player.

Defensive players are required to make verbal calls as they establish position. For example, the player guarding the ball must close out on the shooter and yell "close out."

Defenders who are one-pass away assume denial position, and yell "deny" three times. Defensive players who are two-passes away, assume proper help position by yelling "help" three times.

You want your defenders to front the offensive center when the ball is below the free-throw line. In this situation, your center will yell "front."

When starting this drill at mid-court, you're trying to teach "on-the-line" and "up-the-line" defensive principles. Verbal calls are still required of the defense.

Offensive Rules, Rebounding

Place restrictions on the offense early in the season when running this drill. Start by having your offense stay stationary with no dribbling, screening or cutting. Progress as the defense improves their block-out technique and the offense improves on offensive rebounding.

If the offensive team scores (1 point), they immediately apply a full-court, 2-2-1 press, which denies the inbound pass. The fact that a steal is given 2 points provides added incentive to the pressing team.

The defensive team can press, steal and score as many points as possible. The team on offense must execute their press-break offense and get a good shot off to complete their turn. This allows both teams to practice your press and press offense in a very competitive setting.

After the offense breaks the press and gets a shot off, if the defensive team secures a rebound (2 points), they should immediately run a fast break and attempt to score (1 point).

Drill Options

You might want to start this drill by stating to your players that a good shot, made or missed, ends the possession. In our situation, we make the varsity score a basket, while the junior varsity team only has to get a good shot to end the possession. Once the possession ends, the drill continues with the teams reversed.

Each team will get three repetitions on offense and defense before the drill ends.

8-SECOND CHARGE DRILL

By Will Mayer, Head Boys Coach,
Middletown North High School, Middletown, N.J.

This is an excellent drill to get your players in the habit of using proper footwork and learning the intricacies of defensive positioning. Set up a line of offensive players on the sideline at each hash mark (each player has a ball) and position a line of defensive players on each baseline.

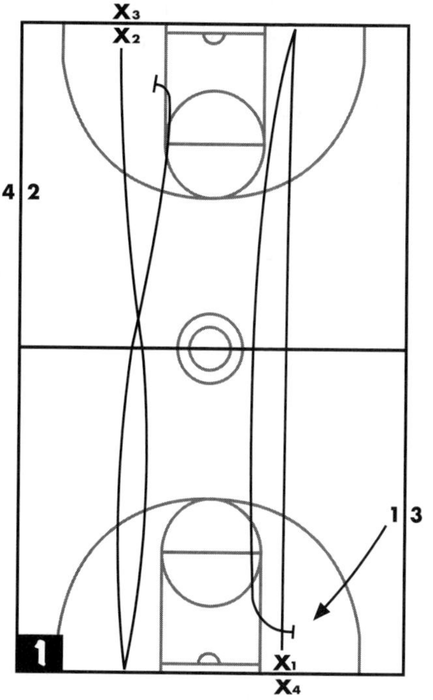

to the opposite low block. Once the defender gets back to the low block, he or she must quickly get into proper defensive position, trying to draw a charge from the oncoming offensive player who's dribbling hard from the hash mark for a left-handed layup. The defenders have 8-seconds to get downcourt, back to the low block and into proper defensive position. The coach verbally counts down the seconds out loud. The offensive player begins his or her drive at the 5- or 4-second mark.

You may have to modify the times for this drill, depending on the age, speed and ability of your players. X1 and O1 quickly switch positions and the drill is repeated. Run the drill for as long as you need to.

DIAGRAM 1: *8-Second Charge Drill.*
On the coach's signal, X1 and X2 must sprint to the opposite baseline, touch it and then run all the way back

"5-ON-5-FOR-5" DRILL

By Will Mayer, Head Boys Coach,
Middletown North High School, Middletown, N.J.

Here's a great drill to use as a practice finisher or for executing your set plays in a live, game-like situation.

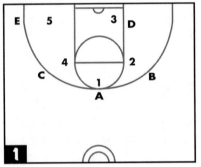

DIAGRAM 1: *5-On-5-To-5.* Play 5-on-5 half court for five consecutive possessions, then switch offense to defense and play another five posses-

sions. The coach keeps score and the losing team runs. The offensive players are not allowed to freelance, and must run either the offense or set plays that your team is going to use in your next game. Same goes for the defense.

Add the following scoring system into the drill to make the "little things" for proper execution more valuable.

❖ Defensive stop = 1 point.
❖ Made field goal = 1 point.
❖ Drawing a charge = 2 points.
❖ Offensive rebound = 1 point.
❖ Forcing a turnover = 2 points.

Two Shooting Ring Drills

By David Rappi, Head Boys Coach,
Hutchinson-Central Tech High School, Buffalo, N.Y.

Here are two shooting drills that also incorporate other valuable skills such as rebounding from the weak side, boxing out and outlet passing.

Weak-Side Rebound Drill:

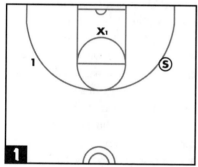

DIAGRAM 1: *Shooting Drill 1 — Weak-side Rebound Drill (A).* For this drill, have three players to a basket — a shooter from the wing (S), a defender positioned in the lane (X1) in help-side position and an offensive player on the weak-side wing area (1).

DIAGRAM 2: *Shooting Drill 1 — Weak-side Rebound Drill (B).* When the shooter takes a shot, X1 calls out "Shot!" and boxes out. 1 crashes the boards from the weak side. X1 must watch the shot, while keeping an eye on the incoming rebounder, initiating contact and maintaining proper box-out position.

Use a scoring system, where 1

point is awarded for every made shot, 2 points for a defensive rebound and 3 points for an offensive rebound from the weak side.

The shooter takes two shots from the wing and then all players rotate positions clockwise. Games are up to 7 points. The losing players owe you 10 push-ups. Run this drill for 7 to 10 minutes, getting in as many games as you can in that timeframe.

R.O.P.S. (Rebound, Outlet, Post & Score) Drill:

DIAGRAM 3: *Shooting Drill 2 — R.O.P.S. Drill (A).* Place two players in the paint (X's), a coach at the free-throw line (C), two shooters at the top of the key (S) and two wing players set up wide on each wing area (W).

The coach initiates the action by throwing a ball off the backboard or rim. The two players in the lane battle for the rebound. Whichever player

secures the rebound immediately becomes and offensive post player and must throw an outlet pass to the nearest wing player.

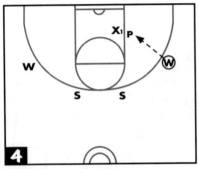

DIAGRAM 4: *Shooting Drill 2 — R.O.P.S. Drill (B).* As P and X battle for position in the ball-side low post, the wing player attempts to feed the post with an entry pass. The players continue play (even on made shots,

they must fight for the ball as it comes through the net) until the coach decides to rotate the players or for a set number of baskets.

DIAGRAM 5: *Shooting Drill 2 — R.O.P.S. Drill (C).* When the coach yells "Switch!" the shooters (S) exchange position with the wing players (W). When the ball is fed back out to the shooters, he or she can shoot the jumper or feed the post.

Once a jump shot is taken, the two post players again battle for position and whoever secures the ball — on a make or rebounded miss — becomes the offensive post player, and he or she must throw the outlet to the nearest player on the wing and the drill resumes.

COMPETITIVE 1-'

By Craig Mellendorf, Head Gu .
Martin Luther High School, Greenda.

Divide your team into two lines of players (X's and O's) and position a line at each free-throw lane line out of bounds, under the basket. The first player in each line steps to the nearest low block. A coach stands at the top of the key with a basketball.

DIAGRAM 1: The coach initiates the drill by setting the ball down on the floor and quickly backs up to half court. As soon as the ball touches the floor, the players on each low block must execute a quick defensive slide to the nearest sideline, touch it and sprint to get the ball. Whoever retrieves the ball first is on offense and the players immediately play 1-

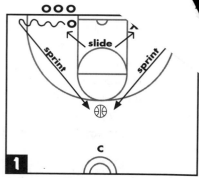

on-1 until a basket is scored.

The losing players runs a lap and the next two players in line step up to each low block to run the drill again. Continue the drill for a predetermined time limit.

MAN-WEAVE-TO-2-ON-2 DRILL

David Clyde, Head Boys Coach,
Sam Houston High School, Arlington, Texas

Here's an effective team drill that transforms from a 3-man weave against a defender into a 2-on-2 drill. Divide your team into three lines of players and position them evenly across the mid-court line. Place one defender at the top of the key.

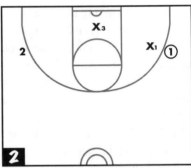

DIAGRAM 2: *2-On-2 Game.* Immediately after 2 has taken his or her shot, the rebound is outletted to either 1 and 2 and a game of 2-on-2 ensues with 1 and 2 playing against X1 and X3.

After the 2-on-2 game, player 1 rotates to defense and the drill is repeated. Continue to rotate players and run the drill for as long as you wish.

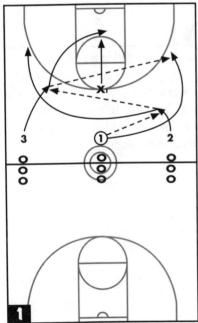

DIAGRAM 1: *3-Man Weave (Vs. A Defender).* Run the 3-man weave against the defender. The weave should be run so that 2 is the last player to touch the ball and shoots a layup or jump shot. Players X and 3 fight for the rebound.

"17 Seconds" I

By Richard Dardenne, Basketball
Northeast Christian Academy, Kingwood, -

Here's a terrific drill to develop trapping abilities and defensive footwork among your defensive players, as well as working on transition offense and getting your players used to passing the ball while under heavy defensive pressure.

Position the players as shown in Diagram 1, with a coach inbounding the ball on the baseline.

inbounds the ball to player 1. X1 and X2 immediately sprint at 1 to form a double-team trap. 1 must hold the ball until the double-team arrives.

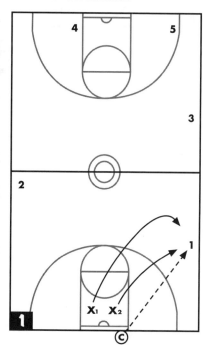

DIAGRAM 1: Place two defenders (X1 and X2) on the baseline and have them try to disrupt the inbounding of the ball by the coach. The coach

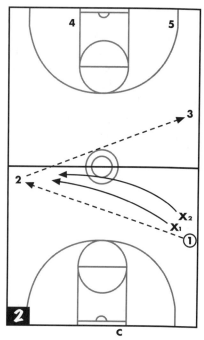

DIAGRAM 2: Player 1 passes out of the double-team to 2 and the two defenders, X1 and X2, sprint to quickly form a double-team trap on 2. 2 must wait for the double-team to arrive before he or she can pass to 3.

2 passes to 3 out of the double-team and the two defenders sprint toward 3 to form a double-team trap.

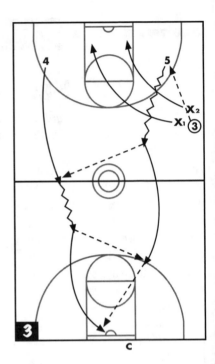

or the double-team to
re passing to either 4 or 5.
M 3: 3 passes out of the dou-
am to either 4 or 5. Once 4 or 5
e the ball, they begin a quick 2-on-
0 fast-break transition going the other
way downcourt, passing the ball back-
and-forth until they make a layup.

The players' goal is to do the entire
drill in under 17 seconds! Come up with
a "rewards system" for any deflections,
forced turnovers or steals that X1 and
X2 get so that they have incentive to
double-team to the best of their abilities.

After the drill is completed, rotate
the players so that X1 and X2 become
4 and 5, 4 and 5 become the two new
defenders on the baseline facing the
coach, and 1 and 2 assume the spots
that 2 and 3 had in the original positioning of the drill.

BEHIND-THE-COACH, 1-ON-1 DRILL

By Chris Endres, Assistant Boys Coach,
Cardington-Lincoln High School, Cardington, Ohio

One of the best ways to teach on-the-ball defense and build a competitive edge among your players is with 1-on-1 defensive drills. In these types of drills, players learn the importance of such critical defensive techniques such as maintaining a proper stance with knees bent, setting up in angles to cut off an offensive player's penetration, using proper footwork, keeping the feet moving and fighting through fatigue at the end of a game. We teach these elements through an innovative drill called "Behind-The-Coach, 1-on-1."

Divide your players into two squads (we use "home" and "away" jerseys to separate the team). At one end of the court, on the left side of the basket, place three pairs of players — one player from each "home" or "away" squad per pair — who will be matched up against one another. Do the same thing on the other side of the court, only with the three pairs of players set up on the right side of the basket.

A coach is set up at each hash mark. Put 4 minutes on the gym clock. One player has a ball and is positioned on the baseline, while his or her opponent is set up beside him or her, and ready to play defense.

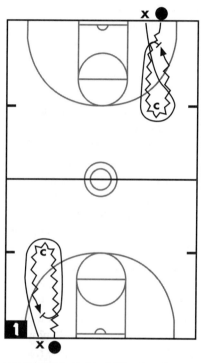

DIAGRAM 1: *Behind-The-Coach, 1-On-1 Drill (A).* On the coach's signal, the clock begins counting down and both players sprint toward the coach, each circling behind him or her. The offensive player crosses around the coach from the baseline side (underneath) and the defensive player curls around the coach from the sideline side (over the top).

Once the players circle around the coach, it becomes a game of 1-on-1.

The offensive player has three dribbles to beat the defender and score. Due to the starting position, the defensive player is forced to hustle, sprint hard to get ahead of the ball handler, gain a proper angle and cut him or her off to stop the scoring attempt. The same action is occurring on both ends of the floor simultaneously.

After the 4 minutes has expired, the offense switches to defense, the clock is reset and the drill is run for another 4 minutes.

The coaches must keep track of how many total points each team (home or away) has scored throughout the 8 minutes of drill action. Count any fouls as 1 point, as this teaches your defenders to play aggressively, yet without fouling. The winning team gets a water break and the losing team has to run sprints or perform push-ups DIAGRAM 2: *Behind-The-Coach, 1-On-1 Drill (B)*. When the players return from the water break or punishment phase, have them switch to the other side of the basket and run the drill again for another 8 minutes total (again switching offense-to-

defense after the 4-minute mark). The second time around, you'll find that this drill becomes quite intense, as players seem to find a stronger mindset to get down into their stance and get after it defensively. When points and punishments are at stake — players become quite competitive and rise to a higher level.

CONTINUOUS FAST-BREAK DRILL

By Troy Pearson, Girls Basketball Coach,
National Director of Dr. Dish Drills & Training, Farmington, Minn.

Here's a great drill to teach your players how to read their options on the fast break and introduce them to fundamental transition principles. This drill calls for a minimum of 15 players, one ball and the entire length of one court.

Divide your team into three groups of five players. Group O1, O2, O3, O4 and O5 set up in a single-file line at the middle of the floor, with two players X1 and X2 in tandem at one of the floor and X6 and X7 stationed on the other end. Players X3, X4 and X 5 line up on one sideline, while X8, X9 and X10 line up on the other sideline. DIAGRAM 1: *Continuous Fast-Break Drill.* The drill begins with O1, O2, O3, O4 and O5 attacking X1 and X2 in a 5-on-2 fast-break situation. Once the ball crosses the midcourt line, X3, X4 and X5 enter the play as defensive trailers on the break.

As soon as they finish attacking that side of the court, the offensive players attack the other side of the floor. Once again, when the ball crosses midcourt, the defenders X8, X9 and X10 come onto the court and hustle down to help in defensive transition. While this is occurring, two other defenders stay under on one end of the floor and three of them go back to

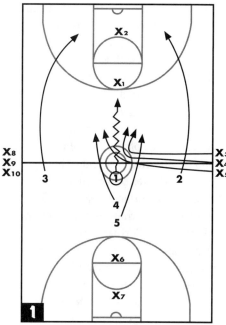

the sideline, returning to help when the offense comes back the other way.

Run this drill for a predetermined amount of time and then rotate the three groups of players clockwise, until each group has had several repetitions on offense. The players must be focused, intense and constantly thinking about their options in transition.

"Braveheart" Rebounding Drill

By J. Eric Stein, Head Boys Coach,
Wheeler School, Providence, R.I.

All coaches face a fair share of frustration when it comes to teaching the skills of aggressive rebounding.

We came up with a combination drill that conditions players to be more physical under the boards. Dubbed the "Braveheart" drill (after Mel Gibson's film of the same name), it has sparked players' excitement about improving rebounding ability.

This drill was conceived to promote the importance of a good box-out technique while promoting clean, physical play. Furthermore, it also combines defensive technique and clearing out of the ball to the outlet players — another key fundamental skill that should be reinforced at every opportunity.

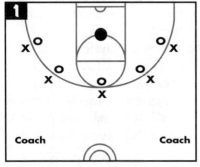

DIAGRAM 1: *Starting Position.* The drill starts with a basketball set on the floor in the middle of the paint.

Players are spread out along the 3-point line in pairs, with their backs to one another. While the diagrams show five players, this drill can be run with as many as nine pairs of players spread out along the 3-point line. Teams are separated by the color of their practice jerseys.

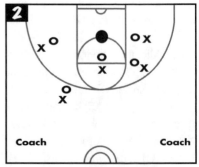

DIAGRAM 2: *"Go" Command.* On the coach's command of "Go!," the players box out each other with a low base while keeping their hands up (reinforcing the "hands up" rebounding form). Players (depending on whether in the inside or outside position) continue to drive each other either closer to the ball or away from it.

DIAGRAM 3: *"Hold" Command.* Meanwhile, the coach will yell "Hold!" (another reference from the Braveheart film that adds an imaginative touch to keep the interest of the players). At this point, the pairs can be in vastly different locations on the court

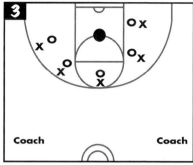

due to the effectiveness of their box outs. When the coach calls "Hold!" for a second time, players break free and race toward the ball.

Encourage players not to dive at the ball or pile on it in this particular drill.

Teaches Defense, Outlet Passing, Too

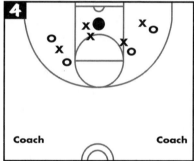

DIAGRAM 4: *Defense, Clear-Out.* Once a player picks up the ball, the drill becomes a defensive game. Drib-

bling is not allowed. The ball may only be advanced through passing. The defensive team, meanwhile, can trap the ball, deny the pass, etc. After getting possession, the rebounding team's objective is to clear the ball to the coach in the outlet area.

DIAGRAM 5: *Ball Cleared To Coach (1 Point).* The team that gains control of the ball and makes a good pass to the outlet earns 1 point. Teams alternate from the inside to outside position after each point scored.

Normally, the first team to score 5 points wins the drill. The losing team usually faces the consequence of 20 wall jumps (quick jumps as high as possible with the hands overhead) or squat-thrusts (regular squat thrust but with two hands as high overhead as possible). These consequences are chosen because they develop the physical skills necessary to become a strong rebounder.

"Fight for your freedom," the lasting words of Braveheart legend William Wallace, have been altered in our gym. Since this drill was implemented, our team hears, "Fight for your rebounds!"

"Scoop Drill" & "Seal Drill"

By Larry Menefee, Head Boys Coach,
Wichita Falls High School, Wichita Falls, Texas

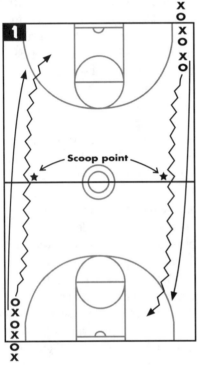

and "scoops" at the basketball in an underhand motion in an attempt to know the ball loose and forward, out of the dribbler's hand. The underhand scoop technique is taught and stressed in this drill — as opposed to slapping down at the ball — because an official will rarely call a foul on a scoop attempt to knock the ball loose.

If the offensive player makes the layup, he or she grabs the ball as it comes out of the net and comes back down the other side of the court. The coach signals the next pair to go, at a staggered pace so the drill remains continuous and that there is always a pair of players sprinting toward each basket.

DIAGRAM 2: *Seal Drill.* The players form a single-file line and the offensive player (the first player in line) attempts to dribble the length of the floor for a layup. A defender (the second player in line) trails closely behind the dribbler, shuffling on the inside of ball handler until he or she reaches the mid-court line. Once the ball handler crosses the mid-court line, the defender's goal is to sprint hard, catch up with the dribbler and force him or her toward the baseline, away from the basket.

DIAGRAM 1: *Scoop Drill.* Set up all your players in a single-file line and arrange so that every other player in line has a basketball. The first player is on offense and the second player is a defender. On the coach's signal, the offensive player dribbles the length of the court with either the left or right hand. The defensive player trails behind the dribbler on the ball side.

As the dribbler nears mid-court, the trailing defender leans forward

Run both of these drills for a prede-

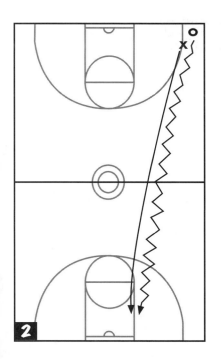

termined set time limit. Keep a close eye on the defender's footwork and make sure that he or she stays under control and utilizes proper defensive technique.

BONUS DRILL: ARMY DRILL

By Brian McCormick, Coach And Director,
High-Five Hoop School, Sacramento, Calif.

THIS IS A VERY simple drill and can be used in a number of different ways to cover multiple situations. Line up two teams of five players across from each other, one on the baseline (offense) and one on the free-throw line (defense). The coach throws a ball to any one of the five offensive players to begin transition downcourt. When the pass is thrown, the corresponding defensive player must run and touch the baseline and then get back into the play. The other defensive players must retreat, communicate and try to slow the progress of the ball. The offensive players must get the ball downcourt as quickly as possible to take advantage of the 5-on-4 situation.

At any point in the drill, the coach can yell out a defensive player's name and that player must run from wherever they are on the court and go touch the baseline and then return to the action. This allows the offense other temporary advantages, such as a 5-on-3 break.

This drill can be set up with as many people as needed to work on other types of transition situations (2-on-1s, 3-on-1s, 4-on-2s, etc.).

100 TRIPS DRILL — THE FULL-COURT WORKOUT

By Ed Andrist, Head Mens Coach,
University of Wisconsin — Stout, Menomonie, Wis.

This workout is designed for your players to get out and get after it on the full-court level. It's an intense workout that can be completed in about 35 minutes with the help of a rebounder, partner or coach.

With this workout we hope to accomplish the following:

❖ Develop the ability to push the ball and go full speed.

❖ Work on scoring off the dribble.

❖ Practice going by defenders in the open court and body-to-body.

❖ Conditioning.

❖ Get better by practicing the way we are going to play.

Drill Execution

1. Each drill is done by executing four full court trips. A trip is one length of the court.

2. Every drill will start on the baseline or on the block. On any type of long rebound, go and get the ball and restart on the baseline or block, whichever the drill specifies.

3. Determine what type of shot you want to work on. End each trip with a three pointer, a pull-up jumper or a layup. Vary the workout to keep it interesting.

4. After every four trips you will shoot four free throws to rest. It's important to rest between every four trips in order to be able to execute the drills at game speed. During the workout you will shoot 100 free throws.

5. The workout goes faster if you have a rebounder chase down long rebounds and free throws. Some drills require a partner to hold a broom to act as a defender or to catch passes. Modify the drills accordingly if without a partner.

6. Use your creativity to modify the workout. Substitute moves you want to work on or need help with. Split the workout if needed, 50 trips in the morning and 50 in the afternoon. Fit the workout to your schedule.

The Drills

DIAGRAM 1: *2-Ball Drill (Straight).* Start in the corner of the court with two basketballs. Dribble both balls at the same time going from the corner to the elbow, to halfcourt, to the elbow, to the corner. Turn and execute an alternating two-ball dribble on the way back following the same pattern. Repeat the sequence one more time for the first four trips. Shoot free throws.

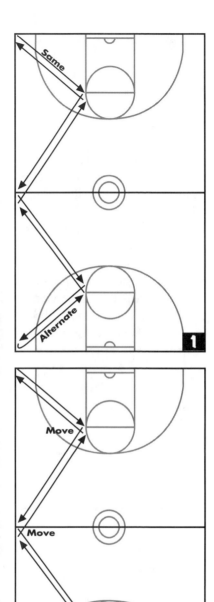

each time you change direction. If you are in the advanced stages of handling two basketballs use a switch, between the legs, behind the back, inside-out or some type of combo move.

A simpler variation of the drill would be to execute the same move each time you change direction, working on the same move until it is mastered. Complete twice, then shoot free throws.

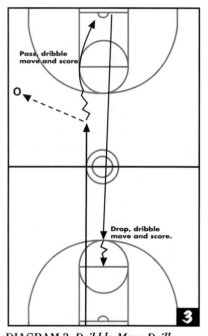

DIAGRAM 3: *Dribble-Move Drill.*
Start on the baseline in the lane with two basketballs. Dribbling both balls at the same time, go hard to the opposite three point line and just let one of the balls go. Execute a hard stutter and then a strong dribble move (cross-over, between legs, behind back, etc.) and score. Turn around and retrieve the ball that was dropped.

Execute the same drill on the way

DIAGRAM 2: *Sean Miller Drill (w/ move)* This time when you execute the drill you will use a different move back, but this time when you are 5 to 10 feet from the three point line make a pass to your partner. Immediately after making the pass make a hard stutter and strong dribble move, take the ball to the basket and score. Repeat the sequence down and back and shoot free throws.

Push Dribble (Right Hand)

Our goal is to go the length of the court in three dribbles by pushing the ball out in front without carrying or traveling. Start on the baseline in the lane, go the length of the court and lay it in. Repeat the sequence three more times with right hand. Shoot four free throws.

Push Dribble (Left Hand)

Same drill sequence using the left hand on all four trips. Shoot free throws.

moves. Each move is done on a separate four trips up the court (24 total), two trips with the right hand and two trips with the left hand working on the same move. Each trip starts on the baseline.

Push the ball out in front and get to the opposite three point line (in three dribbles). Execute the move and try to get to the basket with only one dribble.

The six moves we work on in this series are: hard stutter and explode to basket, hard stutter and cross over dribble, inside out or fake cross over, between the legs, behind the back, combination or combo move. Shoot free throws after each sequence.

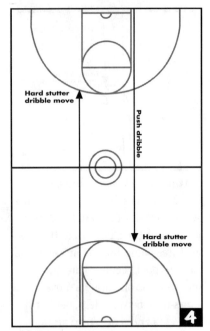

DIAGRAM 4: *Push, Stutter Series.* In this series we work on six different

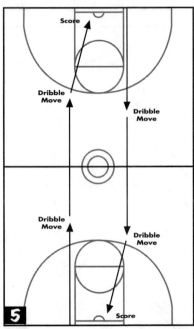

DIAGRAM 5: *Donovan Drill.* Once again we are working on the same sequence of drills as in the push stutter series. Start on the block and exe-

cute the dribble move at each hash mark. Each move is performed twice on the way down and twice on the way back, two trips right handed and two trips left handed. Shoot free throws after each sequence.

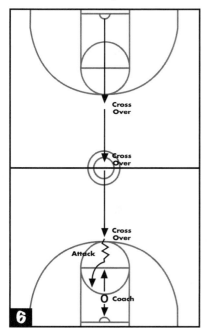

DIAGRAM 6: Hurley Drill. Start on the baseline in the lane and go hard to the basket. Execute three cross over dribbles, one at the top of the key, one at halfcourt and the other above the key on the opposite end of the floor. The coach, partner or rebounder lines up in the opposite lane with a broom. Attack the defender in the lane simulating an attack from a tall defender. If the defender doesn't come out and challenge the dribbler, pull up and shoot the jumper. If challenged, take the ball hard to the basket and look to score. Repeat this sequence seven more

times (two sets of four trips). Shoot free throws after each sequence.

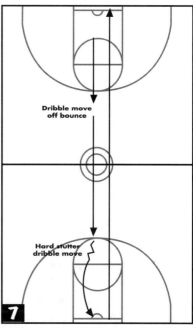

DIAGRAM 7: *Off-The-Board Drill.* The player starts in the lane facing the basket. Throw the ball hard off the backboard so it goes over their head. The player should turn and get to the ball, execute a dribble move off the initial bounce and take the ball hard to the opposite three point line. Perform a hard stutter and dribble move and score. Quickly take the ball out of the net and push dribble the length of the court on the way back (try to make it in three dribbles). We do this in two sets of four trips, shooting free throws after each set.

DIAGRAM 8: *Full-Court, Hard-Move Series.* In this series (the same six moves as in the Push Stutter and Donovan series) each dribble move is performed with the weak hand only.

Each of the moves is performed at half court, once on the way down and once on the way back. There are six moves, so this series will add up to 12 full court trips. The sequence is hard stutter with weak hand, stutter and cross over weak to strong hand, inside out or fake cross over, between the legs weak hand to strong, behind the back weak hand to strong and a combo move initiated with the weak hand. Shoot free throws after every four trips.

Imagination Dribble

In this drill, instruct the players to imagine that they are being defended by someone quick. They must go the length of the court executing any sequence of moves they want.

Have some fun with this drill and put together some tough dribble combinations. It's a good idea to have the players shoot free throws after they run this drill, as they'll be pretty well fatigued.

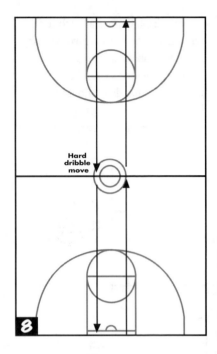

Hard
dribble
move

8

RUN-AND-DOUBLE DRILL

By Brent Bell, Head Boys Coach
Woodberry Forest School. Woodberry Forest, Va.

The Three-On-Three vs. Run-And-Double Drill is successful for several reasons. The drill incorporates aspects of pressure defense, trapping, beating traps, fast-break situations and recovery.

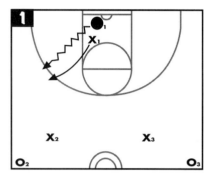

OFFENSIVE EMPHASIS

❖ Attacking pressure and making a decisive play before the double-team comes.

❖ Making players a target for a pass in the middle of the floor.

❖ Executing a two-on-one break.

DEFENSIVE EMPHASIS

❖ Forcing the ball to the sideline and trapping.

❖ Understanding the role of an interceptor on defense.

❖ Recovering quickly once a trap is beaten.

DRILL SPECIFICS

❖ Full-court with 12 players grouped in four sets of three players.

❖ Two players, one offensive and one defensive, start under the basket.

❖ Four players, two offensive and two defensive, start at midcourt.

DIAGRAM 1: Group 1 begins with its ball handler trying to push the ball up the floor. The player guarding the ball handler pushes him or her to the sideline and into the double-team.

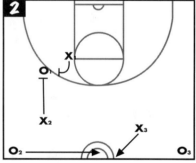

DIAGRAM 2: As the defender commits to the double-team, the offensive player he or she is guarding should sprint to the middle of the court. Have that player touch the center circle.

DIAGRAM 3: The ball handler passes to the player in the middle before the trap arrives. When the opposite defender sees his or her teammate move to the double-team, that defender should move to the middle of the floor and try to become an interceptor.

Once the ball is caught in the middle, a two-on-one fast break can be run with the three players hustling to get in the play.

Once a basket is made or the defense gets a stop, the next six players try it. Then the drill repeats in the opposite direction with players switching offensive and defensive responsibilities.

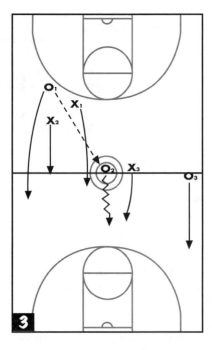

BONUS DRILL: 3-ON-3 HELP-OUT GAME

By Peter Harris, Head Mens Coach
Kansas City College & Bible School, Overland Park, Kan.

THIS DRILL IS RUN with only three players per team. They set up at the point and both wings with the other team picking them up man-to-man. The ball is at the point.

When the ball is passed to a wing, the person guarding the receiver must allow him or her to drive to the hoop to simulate getting beat off the drive. This forces the opposite wing defender to help out.

At this point, the offense is allowed to make two passes before shooting.

THREE POSSIBILITIES OCCUR:

❒ If the help defense is quick enough, they may be able to avoid switching and still stop the drive.
❒ Both defenders may decide to stay and trap the ball.
❒ They may be forced to switch.

This game should be played to a certain number of possessions per team.

(Note: If the help defense is too slow, the dribbler may take the layup).

5-BALL DRILL

By Jim Blaine, Head Boys Coach
Benton High School, Benton, Wis.

The 5-ball drill is a continuous drill that can look like chaos, but really has some outstanding game-like action. It is an especially good drill if you are a transition team.

Position Counts

The key to simplifying the drill for your players is to remind them that the post players will always be in the two post lines (baseline just outside the backboard), the wing players will always be in the wing lines (sideline at mid-lane), and the guards will always be in the guard lines (sideline at hashmark).

When they complete the drill on one end of the court they go to their designated line on the other end. You need at least nine players to run the drill. The circled players start with the balls. **DIAGRAM 1:** To initiate the drill the post player #1 (P1) tosses the ball off the backboard, rebounds it, and outlets to guard #1 (G1). As this is taking place, wing player #1 (W1) takes off down the sideline. G1 makes a dribble move to mid-court, throws a lead pass to W1 and moves to the free throw circle. W1 receives the pass, shoots a jump shot or makes a dribble move to the basket (whatever you designate). After throwing the outlet pass, P1

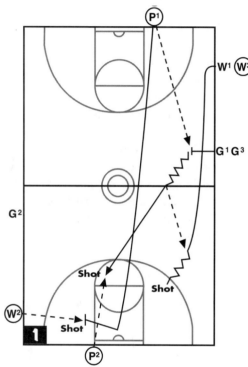

sprints to the opposite block and receives a pass from W2 and performs a post move. P2 passes to G1 at the free throw circle for a jump shot. **DIAGRAM 2:** There should be three balls waiting to be rebounded. P2 grabs one of the loose balls and starts the drill going the other way with an outlet pass to G2. The three players that just had shots go to their perspective lines and the two remaining balls are returned to the post and the wing lines.

Points Of Emphasis

Make sure the guards are catching the outlet pass with their butt to the sideline and are facing up court before they put the ball on the floor. Attack them with a coach to help them form this habit. The post players must sprint and put their head on the rim before sliding to the post. If possible, we have a coach bump them as they try to post up and score. The wings must stay wide when running the floor to see the whole floor before they make a decision to shoot or dribble. Use a coach to run at them or lay back and make them shoot the jumper.

This drill incorporates numerous offensive skills on the move. Passing, catching, shooting, running the floor and conditioning are all taught and the players like the drill because they all get to shoot.

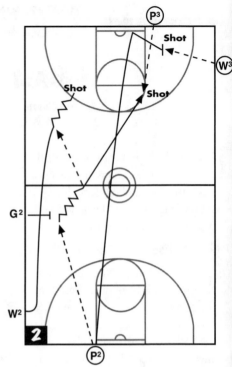

DEFENSIVE DENIAL DRILL

By Alex Allen, Boys Head Coach,
Mohawk High School, Marcola, Ore.

The Defensive Denial Drill is used to allow players to work on three important defensive skills:

1. Denying the pass from the point to the wing.

2. Denying the ball from the corner to the wing and the post.

3. Using the chest to fend off the offensive player as he or she makes a ball-side cut and deny him or her the ball.

This drill gives your players the opportunity to work on one-on-one defensive and offensive skills. Plus, this drill can be done in 5 to 10 minutes.

The drill begins with the coach holding the ball at the point with players at positions 1 to 5. Emphasize to players they must be intense on defense and that offensive players must make the defenders work hard. The first defensive player (X) will start by denying the pass from the point to the wing.

DIAGRAM 1: Player 1 V-cuts back and forth from the wing to the block. The coach (C) passes to 1 three or four times either at the wing or by attempting the backdoor pass. Once the defender knocks down a couple passes, the coach should pass the ball to 2 in the corner.

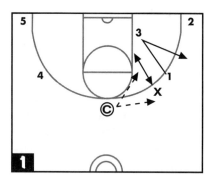

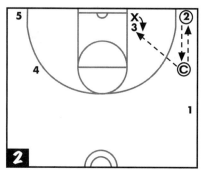

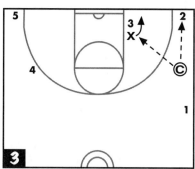

DIAGRAMS 2 AND 3: The coach passes to 2, who moves to the wing as 1 steps aside. Pass the ball to 2 three or

four times and attempt a few passes to 3. The defender covers 3, who is posting up depending on whether the ball is in the corner or at the wing.

This portion of the drill depends upon your offensive and defensive philosophies. We have had our players three-quarters front the post, playing above the post when the ball is above the free-throw line extended and below the post when the ball is below the free-throw line.

When post defense is carried out in this manner, it is critical that the defender move to the front of the post player, not behind the player, when the ball is passed from the wing to the corner or vice versa.

the ball, he or she can go one-on-one with the defender.

DIAGRAM 4: While the defender covers 3, the ball is reversed from 2, to the coach, to 4 and then to 5. As the ball is reversed, the defender must adjust accordingly and move into the help-side position.

DIAGRAM 5: After 5 has the ball for a second or two, 3 cuts hard to the ball at the low or high post. The defender must chest 3 off as the cut to the ball is made.

Make sure 3 is forced to the wing to receive the ball from 5. Once 3 has

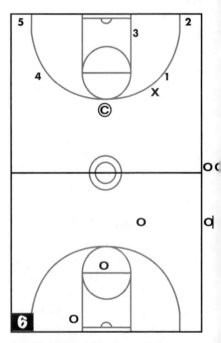

DIAGRAMS 6: Players rotate in numerical order with the defender becoming 1, the next player in line becoming the defender and 5 joining other players shooting free throws.

If you have enough room and coaches, this drill can be run at both ends of the court.

DEVELOPING AGGRESSIVE PLAY

By Tom Piotrowski, Head Girls Coach,
Absegami High School, Absecon, N.J.

One of the peculiar ironies I've encountered in the transition from player to coach deals with aggressive basketball play. As a maturing seven-footer in high school, college and eventually the pros, the biggest problem with my game was that it always seemed to be in first gear.

Coaches screamed and even begged me to step up the intensity.

As I've journeyed into coaching, it is now me who must push the button on the players, screaming and begging for intensity.

My solution involves a proactive approach, as well as a practical design. This article discusses a few of the ways we deal with lazy play. We use this approach with the entire team and individuals as well.

INTRODUCE "AGGRESSIVE" GOALS FORMALLY, IN A SETTING THAT CLEARLY IDENTIFIES THE AIM AND BENEFIT.

❖ Sometimes passionate coaches blitz players with directives in practice, ignoring the personal learning needs of each player. We then wonder why the player acts as if they had never heard us in a game situation.

❖ Accomplish this through private meetings, mailings in the off season and player self-analysis.

IDENTIFY SPECIFIC "AGGRESSIVE" GOALS FOR TEAMS AND INDIVIDUALS.

❖ Team goal: "We will come up with every loose ball."

❖ Individual goal: "I will grab every pass, rebound and loose ball with two hands."

❖ Customized goals for individuals do not always have to be statistically oriented, some can be function oriented. For example, a post player may improve dramatically by simply providing them with concrete reminders to "step to the pass in the post."

REINFORCE "AGGRESSIVE" GOALS IN A CONSISTENT AND POSITIVE MANNER.

❖ Post the goals.

❖ Provide goal sheets and game reports. Include game situations, do's and don't's and your comments. Use quotes, sayings or themes to support the goals.

❖ Use supportive materials. Print articles and use instructional videos when available.

❖ Use post-game video analysis. Have the players chart the fulfillment and failure of goals.

INCORPORATE COMPETITIVE DRILLS INTO PRACTICE.

Obviously, practice sessions must put an exclamation point on any discussion of the how, where and why of being aggressive. The following drills aren't new, but these exercises are our favorites for maintaining aggressive competition in practice.

Whether warming up or working 5-on-5, practice should always move in an orderly, high energy fashion. If you have assistants, they should know the drills, the order of the drills and should help whip up the frenzy during practice.

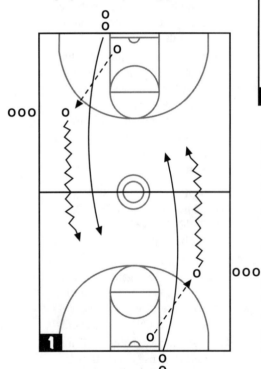

lows. On the outlet pass, the next player in line chases the shooter.

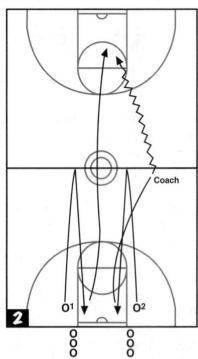

DIAGRAM 2: *Shiner Drill.* The two lines compete against each other. Shorter lines are best. The first two players in line sprint to half court and back, pick up the ball and complete 10 backboard taps. A coach places a third ball somewhere on the open court behind them.

The first player done with the taps races to the ball and starts a drive to the opposite basket. The second player hustles back on defense. The ball is played until scored or rebounded by the defender.

The two players then switch objectives, with the first player racing back on defense to try and stop the second player from driving to the basket.

The ball is played until scored or rebounded by the defender. Have the

DIAGRAM 1: *Full-Court Layups With A Defensive Chaser.* The ball is rebounded off the glass and outlet to the wing. The wing drives to the opposite basket, the rebounder fol-

teams keep score. After one completed trip, the next two in line will go.
DIAGRAM 3: *Go-Go Shooting Drill.* A coach is the passer opposite the shooting line. Place one defender in the middle of the lane and another one down low. The top defender's job is to deny the pass to the shooter.

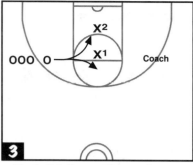

Once the shooter receives the pass, they shoot the jumper or drive to the hoop. The top defender peels off and the low defender attacks the shooter after the pass is completed.

The ball is live until scored or rebounded. Emphasize good offensive footwork and body position to beat the defender to the pass.

BONUS DRILL: 4 DRILL GAMES

By Peter Harris, Head Mens Coach
Kansas City College & Bible School, Overland Park, Kan.

1. NO-HANDS GAME. Too often, players play defense with their hands instead of their feet. This leads to stupid fouls and easy breaks for the opponent. This drill should help break that habit.

The only rule for this game is that the defense must not use their hands in any way unless going for a rebound. Having them grab their own jerseys usually works best because it prevents them from flaring their elbows.

2. NO-DRIBBLE GAME. This drill targets a common problem with team offense — excessive dribbling. Nothing stagnates your offense more than one player dribbling around needlessly.

The only rule for this drill is that the offense can never dribble. You'll be surprised at the intelligent play that suddenly emerges.

3. FREE-THROW GAME. This game emphasizes the importance of free throws. Since many games are won or lost at the line, this game drives home that principle.

This drill begins by having your team run a structured scrimmage. The unique aspect to this game is that when a shot goes in, no points are awarded. Instead, the player earns the privilege of going to the line to earn them by shooting the appropriate number of free throws. If a player misses but is fouled, he or she still goes to the line just as in a real game. In this game, if a team can't hit free throws, they can't score.

4. BOX-OUT GAME. Perhaps nothing gets coaches more riled up in a game than giving up an offensive rebound because of failure to box out.

The simple rule here is that all rebounds are one point (or two if you prefer). Made baskets are scored as normal.

The first time we ran this drill, we allowed no points for made baskets. This really placed the pressure on the rebounding/boxing out. All shots were missed and players were even allowed to score consecutive points by doing several intentional offensive "put-backs," if no one boxed them out.

TRIANGLE-BOX-OUT-AND-GO DRILL

By Mark Graupe, Former Boys Head Coach,
Central High School, Grand Forks, N.D.

For this drill, you need 9, 12 or 15 players divided into groups of three. The players' numbers — 1, 2 and 3 on one team and A, B and C on the other — correspond to position.

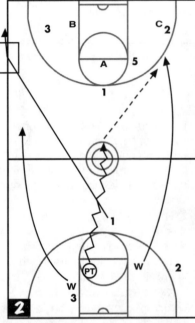

DIAGRAM 1: First the defensive threesome must box out and grab the rebound. The trio must then begin to run the fast break in the opposite direction as 1 passes to 3, who drives down the middle of the court. Once the ball crosses half-court, the defensive point guard, stationed to the left,

takes off and helps the other two defenders. Momentarily, this is a 3-on-2 drill.

DIAGRAM 2: When the point guard and two wings get the rebound at the other end of the court, they fast break the other way toward three new defenders. Three other defenders take the court to begin the drill. The fast-breaking team always takes a 3-point shot to force a wild rebound in the drill.

THREE-IN-A-ROW DRILL

By Mark Graupe, Former Boys Head Coach,
Central High School, Grand Forks, N.D.

This is an intense rebounding drill that should not be run the day before a game due to the chance of an injury.

The defensive player must grab three rebounds in a row to finish the drill.

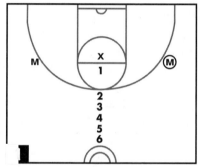

DIAGRAM 1: X is the defensive player. Other teammates form the offensive line of rotating players. Team managers take positions on the wings outside the three-point line.

DIAGRAM 2: The manager on the right takes a shot that is purposely missed.

DIAGRAM 3: If the rebound is grabbed by the defensive player, a pass is made to the manager at the opposite wing position. The defender then hustles over to take a defensive position in front of the next offensive player in line.

The drill continues as the manager moves to the left side of the basket and repeats the action.

INTENSE FREE-THROW DRILLS

By Mike Kindred, Head Girls Coach
Montgomery County High School, Mt. Sterling, Ky.

Coaches are always looking for a better way to keep free-throw shooting intense and competitive. The following two free throw drills, which we incorporate into our practice daily, helped our girls' team shoot 70.5 percent from the line last season.

"Conquer" Fosters Competition

The first drill is called "Conquer." We divide our players into groups of three and place one group at each of the available baskets. While one player is shooting, another player rebounds and the last player runs wind sprints the length of the floor.

The shooter must make a one-and-one. Once he or she has accomplished this, the players rotate their positions. The shooter becomes the runner, the rebounder becomes the shooter and the runner rotates to the rebounding position.

To make the drill more competitive, a time limit is usually imposed and a free throw chart is kept on each group. The losing groups are given additional running depending on their order of finish.

"Free-Throw Train" Rewards Success

Another free-throw shooting drill we have integrated into our practice structure is called the "Free-Throw Train." We typically use this drill at the end of practice.

We place the players in a single file line with youngest players in the front and the oldest bringing up the rear. The athletes then begin to run around the perimeter of the floor until a coach invites the player in the front of the line to come to the free-throw line and shoot.

While the other players continue to run, the shooter must step to the free throw line and make a one-and-one. If the attempts are successful, the player is finished for the day.

If the player misses, he or she must rejoin the other players at the back of the line and continue to run in the "train" until he or she reaches the front of the line once again and can attempt another free throw.

Some players may never make it out of the "Free-Throw Train" in the designated time, so we have these players stay after practice to shoot additional free throws.

Our players enjoy these drills because they are competitive and fun. They have been the key ingredients to our success at the free-throw line and in our increased level of concentration during games.

SCRAMBLE DRILL

By Mike Mondello, Former Coach,
University of Florida, Gainesville, Fla.

This drill incorporates the often over-looked fundamentals of defensive communication and help-and-recover situations.

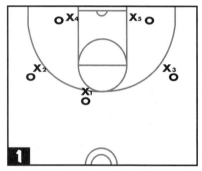

DIAGRAM 1: The drill begins with five offensive and five defensive players in this setup.

Each defensive player is assigned a random number from 1 to 5. The drill is started on the coach's signal. The offense runs your team's plays with the idea of attacking the defense.

DIAGRAM 2: Yell out a number

assigned to one of the defenders. Upon hearing his or her number called, the player must sprint to the half-court line, then scramble back to play defense.

The four remaining teammates must defend the five offensive players until the scrambler returns.

Upon returning, the scrambler can go back to the original defensive assignment or take on another, depending on the position of the other defenders. The other defenders must communicate to prevent an easy score.

The offense should find the open player and attempt to get the ball to that player to score before the defenders can recover. Offensive awareness is the key to finding the open player if the offense is going to score.

To develop continuity, the defense should play through five or six possessions before taking its turn on offense. The drill can be played to a predetermined score or a time limit.

If the defense recovers quickly enough and there was no shot opportunity, another defensive player's number is called and the drill continues. A variation of this drill awards the offense a point for conversion and the defense a point for a stop.

INDEX

Outlet Passing

Passing

Pivots, Pivoting

Screens

Spacing

Team Defense Drills

Transition Drills

LESSITER PUBLICATIONS SHIPPING CHART

ORDER AMOUNT	ECONOMY 5-8 day delivery (shipped USPS)	2-4 DAY DELIVERY (shipped UPS Grnd)	NEXT DAY (shipped UPS next day)	CANADA
Up to $20	$3.95	$7.95	$19.95	$5.95
$21 to $50	$5.95	$8.95	$21.95	$7.95
$51-100	$6.95	$10.95	$24.95	$8.95
$101-$150	$8.95	$12.95	$26.95	$11.95
$151-$200	$9.95	$13.95	$27.95	$13.95
$201 and Up	$11.95	$15.95	$28.95	$15.95

International: Minimum charge $15.75. Orders $51-$300: 25% of total order plus $3 handling charge
Orders over $300: 18% of total plus $3 handling charge. Actual postage charge if amount exceeds 25% or 18% amount.

MAIL TO: *Winning Hoops*, P.O. Box 624, Brookfield, WI 53008-0624
FOR FASTER SERVICE: Call: (800) 645-8455 (U.S. only) or (262) 782-4480
Fax: (262) 782-1252 • **E-mail:** info@lesspub.com • **Web site:** www.winninghoops.com

Basketball Basics

Building Blocks For
Coaching Youth Basketball

*By
Bill Salyers*

Basketball Basics

Building Blocks For Coaching Youth Basketball

Coaching young, inexperienced players or getting into the youth coaching game is one of the hardest things to do in all of basketball. Many coaches have difficulty walking the fine line between delivering information that's overly simple and teaching concepts too complex for young players to grasp. Some coaches just don't know where to begin. These coaches find that building a team from the ground up seems like an intimidating, daunting task that breeds unnecessary stress and anxiety.

Basketball Basics: Building Blocks For Coaching Youth Basketball gives you much-needed guidance and gets you started in the right direction! Authored by nationally respected youth coach and *Winning Hoops* Editorial Advisory Board member Bill Salyers, this 160-page book details the entire process of coaching youth basketball from A-to-Z! Leaving no stone unturned — and jam-packed with detailed diagrams, fundamental drills, game-tested plays and much more — you'll immediately benefit from the highly valuable information on critical youth coaching topics such as:

- Forming And Organizing Your Team
- Setting Rules, Accountability
- Developing A Coaching Philosophy
- Scheduling
- Dealing With Parents And Officials
- Playing Time
- Best Individual and Team Drills
- Game Preparation
- Individual Basics (shooting, passing, dribbling, rebounding, footwork, defense, stretching, etc.)
- Zone Offense (zone theory, "Hawk-eye" offense, attacking gaps, zone specials, etc.)
- Man Offense ("Swing" continuity offense, teaching continuity, etc.)
- Playbook Plays (side out-of-bounds, baseline out-of-bounds, etc.)
- Defense (introduction, rules and teaching the match-up zone)
- Fast Breaks
- And much, more!

A comprehensive look at coaching youth basketball, *Basketball Basics* gives you the real-world tools that you'll need to prepare young players for the journey toward playing high school basketball! Whether you're just starting out or getting back into the youth game, this is a must-have reference book of game-winning coaching knowledge.

160 pages ....Only $19.95

See page 152 for ordering instructions.

Priority Code: WHPPD

Winning Basketball Offense...

From 40 Of America's Winningest Coaches!

The most effective execution of man-to-man, zone, motion, fast-break, flex, shuffle, triangle and press offenses are featured in 200 diagrams and text in this 100-page book from the Winning Hoops editors.

In addition, a special situations chapter shows you how to cash in on three-point shots, inbounds plays, isolation plays and weak-side action plays.

This must-have book is packed with outstanding offenses including:

🏀 Motion	🏀 Press
🏀 Shuffle	🏀 Special Situations
🏀 Man-To-Man	🏀 Triangle
🏀 Flex	🏀 Fast Break
🏀 Zone	🏀 Fundamentals

When it comes to offensive game strategies, nobody diagrams X's and O's better than these 40 coaches. These 40 outstanding contributors have over 400 years of combined basketball coaching experience, including 20 coaches each with over two decades of coaching success.

Don't Delay! Get That Championship Offense Up And Running By Ordering Today!

100 pages ....Only $14.95

See page 152 for ordering instructions.

Priority Code: WHPPD

Add More Power To Your Team's Play!

281 Outstanding Drills Ripped Out Of The Playbooks Of 43 Of The Most Successful Coaches In The Game!

Coming from the playbooks of more than 40 of the most successful coaches in the game, these 55 outstanding drills will improve your ballplayers' skill levels in key areas:

- Ball handling
- Shooting
- Defense
- Rebounding
- Conditioning and Stretching
- Offense
- All-Around Complete Game
- Game Situation
- Mental Toughness
- Transition

Covering all aspects of the game, these drills have been run by some of the game's best coaches and are sure to work for you. Use the innovative drills found in this 100-page book that's jammed with plenty of diagrams to take your team's play to the next level.

Get The Most Out Of Your Practices With This Jam-Packed Book Of Lively Drills! Improve Your Team's Ability To Execute!

100 pages ....**Only $14.95**

See page 152 for ordering instructions.

See page 152 for ordering instructions.

Priority Code: WHPPD

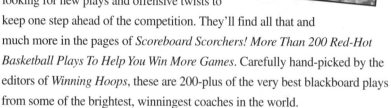

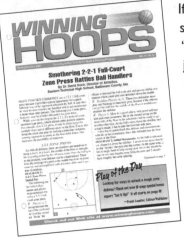